Letter Tracing for Toddlers

3-5 Years

Handwriting, Letter Tracing, Matching, Sight Words, Addition, and Subtraction Activity Book

Part 1

Practice handwriting from 1 to 10, matching numbers with words, counting, and coloring numbers.

Pages 2-32

Name

Trace the number 1 and the word one.

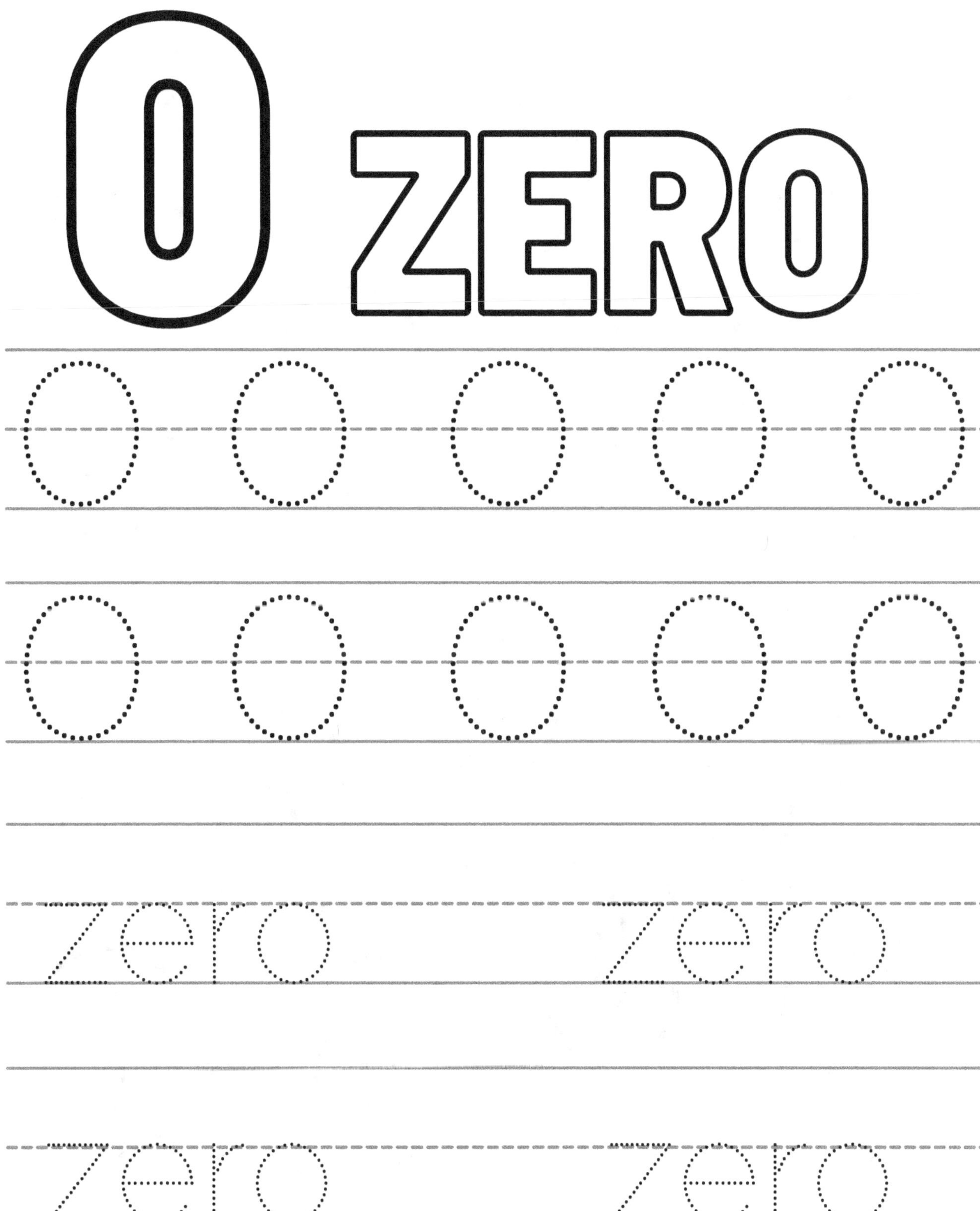

Name_______________

Color all 0 in the picture.

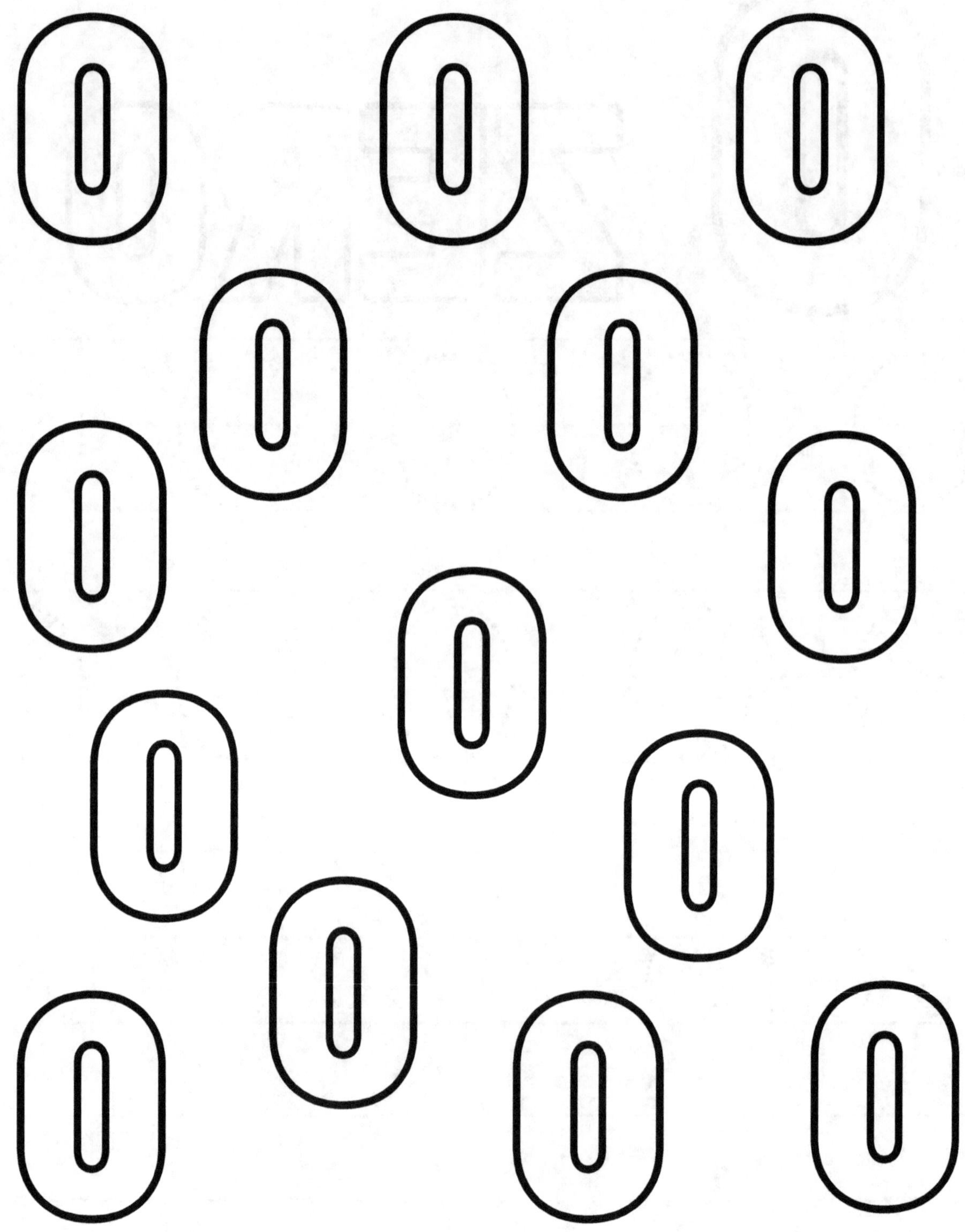

Name

Trace the number 1 and the word one.

1 ONE

Circle 1 BIG fish.

Name

Trace the number 2 and the word two.

2 TWO

2 2 2 2 2

2 2 2 2 2

two two two

two two two

2 TWO

Color 2 turtles.

Name

Trace the number 3 and the word three.

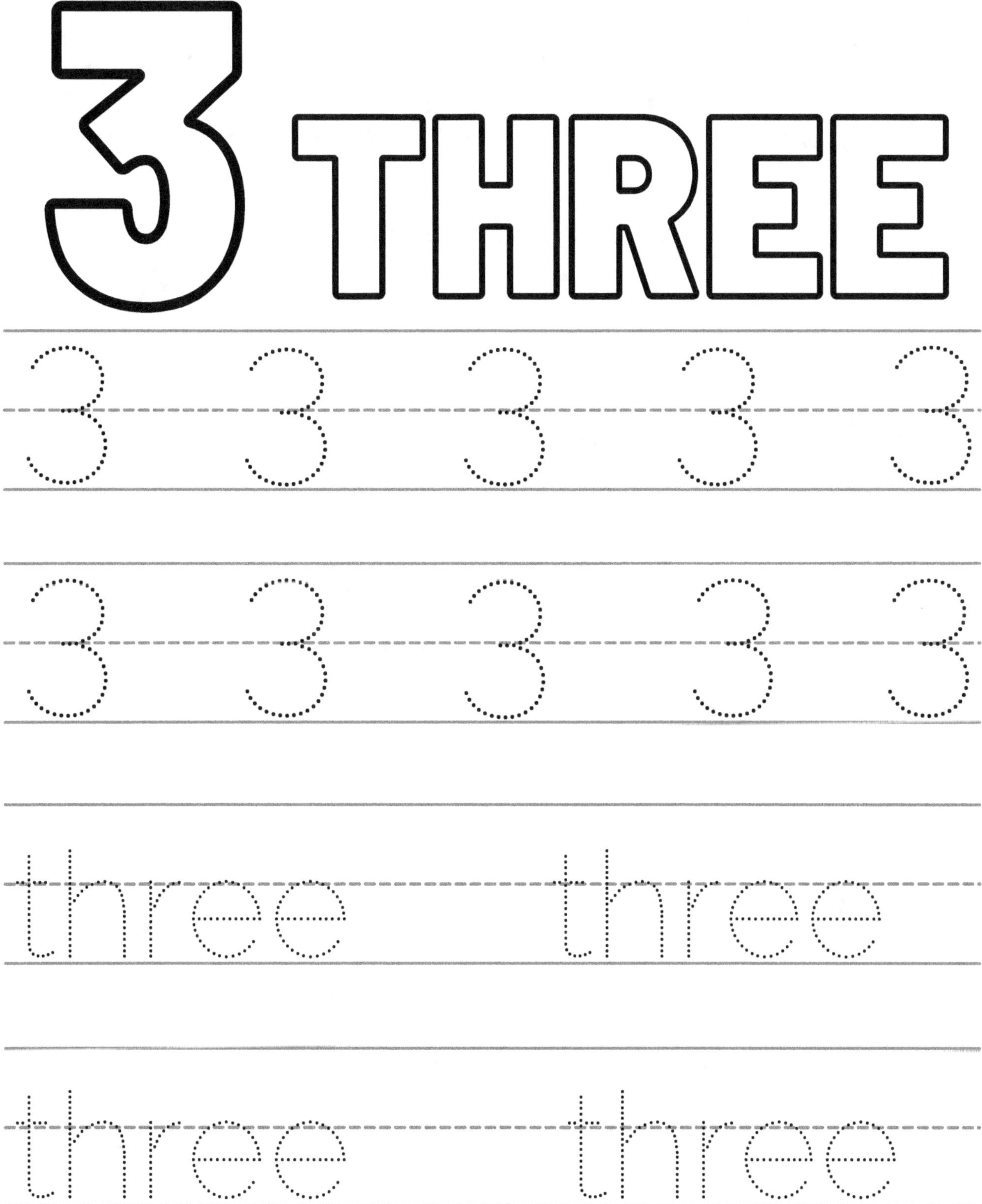

3 THREE

Circle 3 LITTLE stars.

Trace the number 4 and the word four.

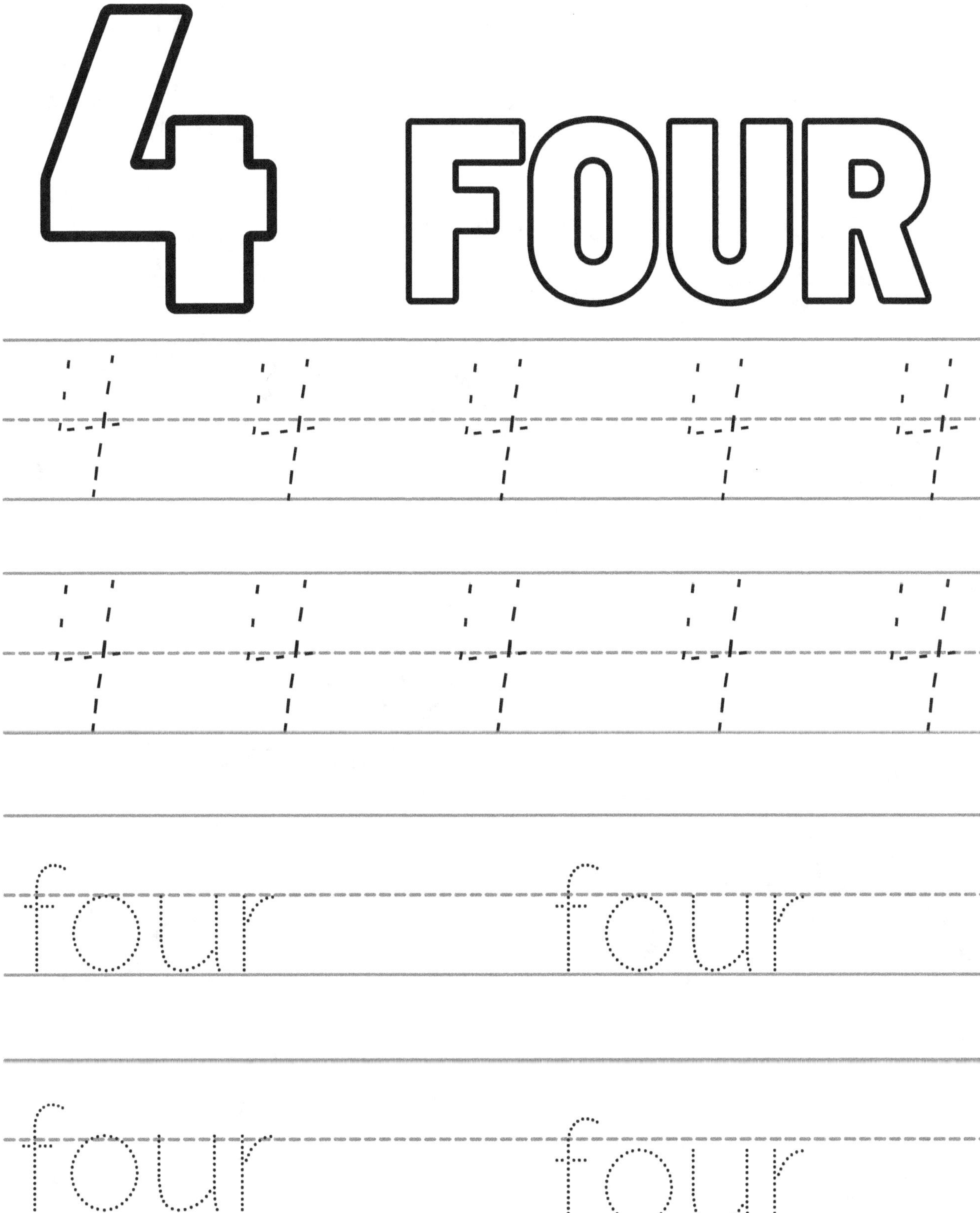

4

FOUR

Name __________________

Color 4 apples.

Name

Trace the number 5 and the word five.

5

Name _______________

FIVE

Color 5 balls.

Name

Trace the number 6 and the word six.

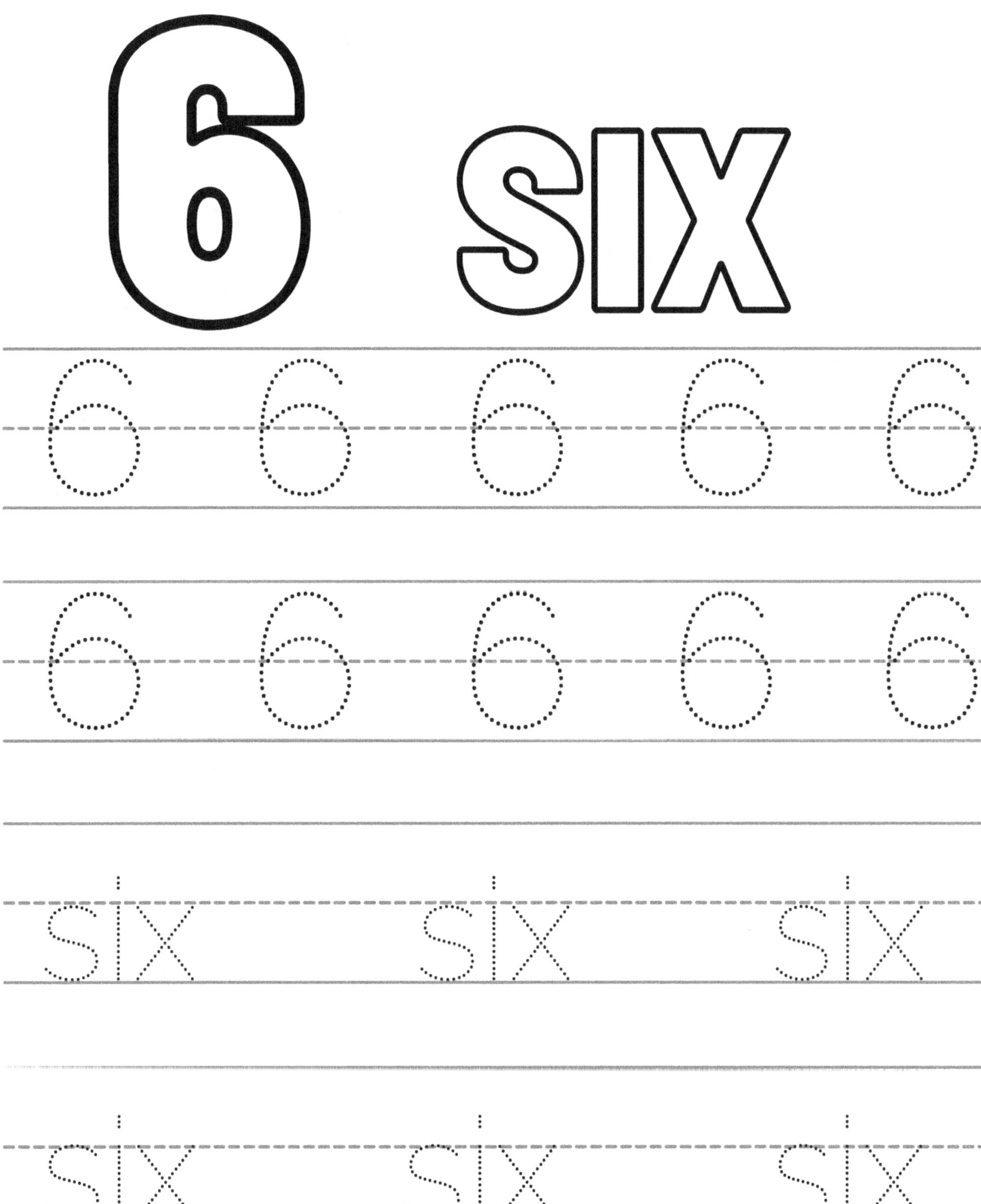

6

Color 6 squares.

Name

Trace the number 7 and the word seven.

7 SEVEN

Circle 7 hearts.

Name

Trace the number 8 and the word eight.

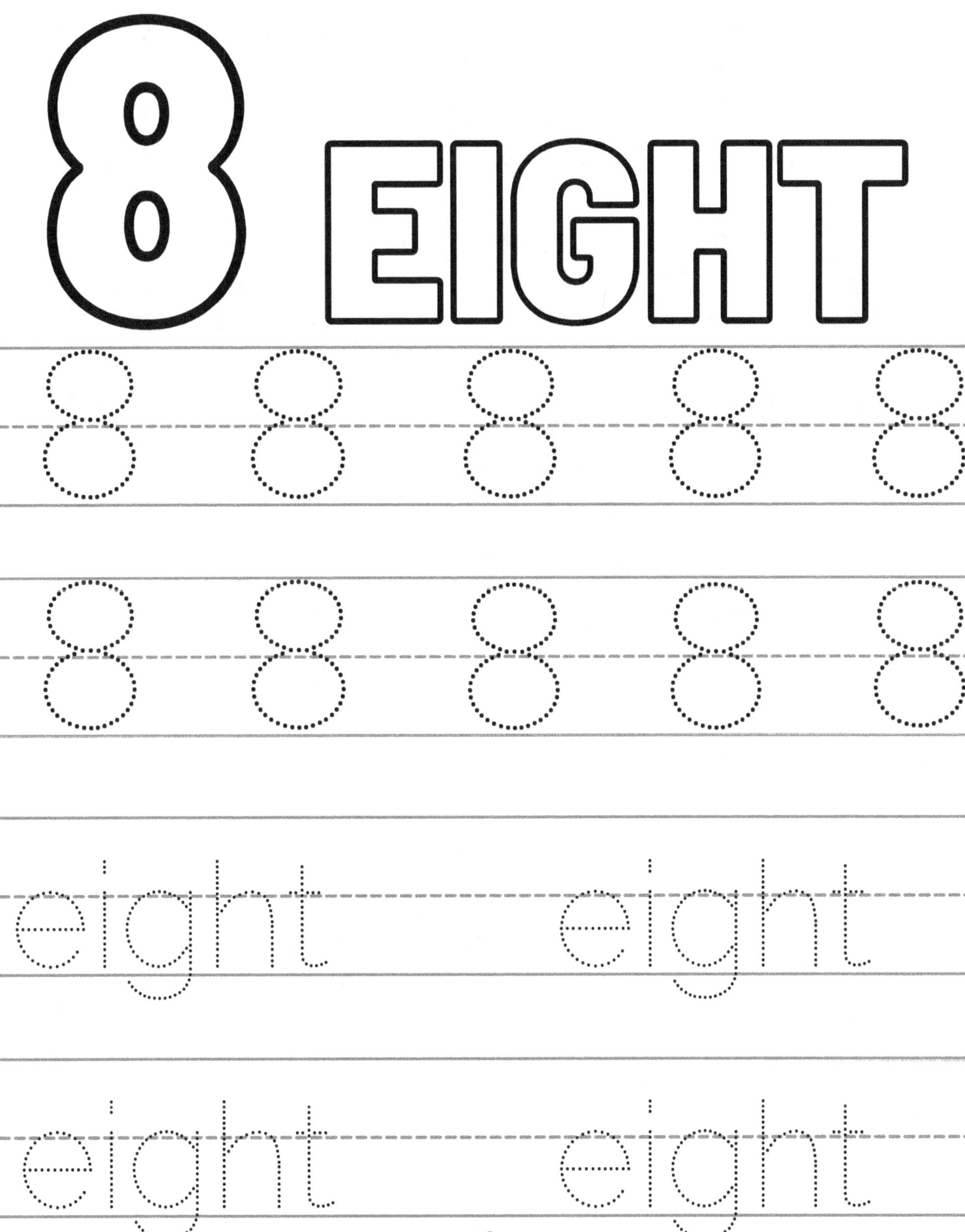

Name ___________________

8 EIGHT

Color 8 cars.

Trace the number 9 and the word nine.

9 NINE

Circle 9 nines.

Trace the number 10 and the word ten.

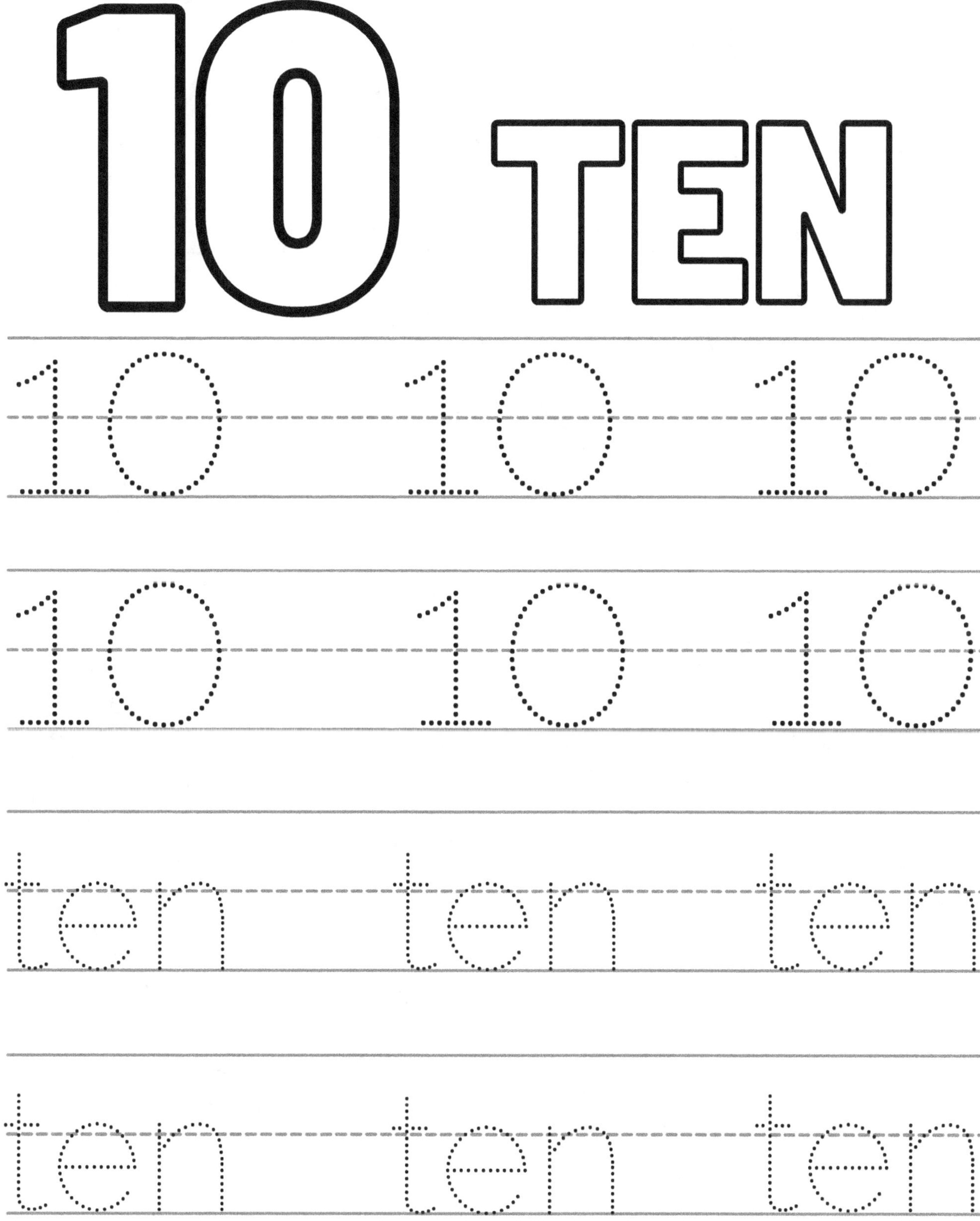

10

TEN

Name

Color 10 bats.

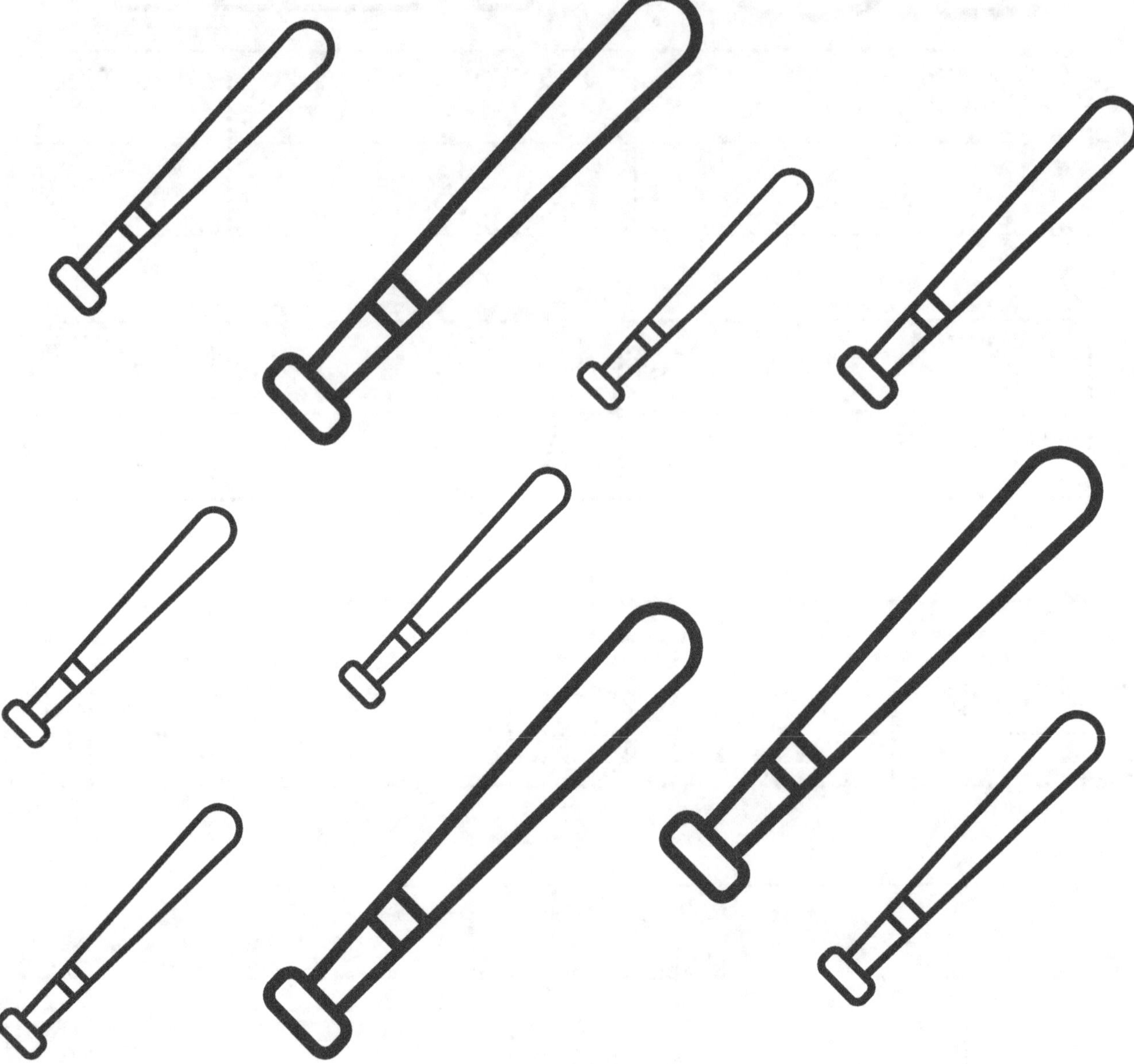

Name

Trace the numbers from 1 to 5

1 2 3 4 5

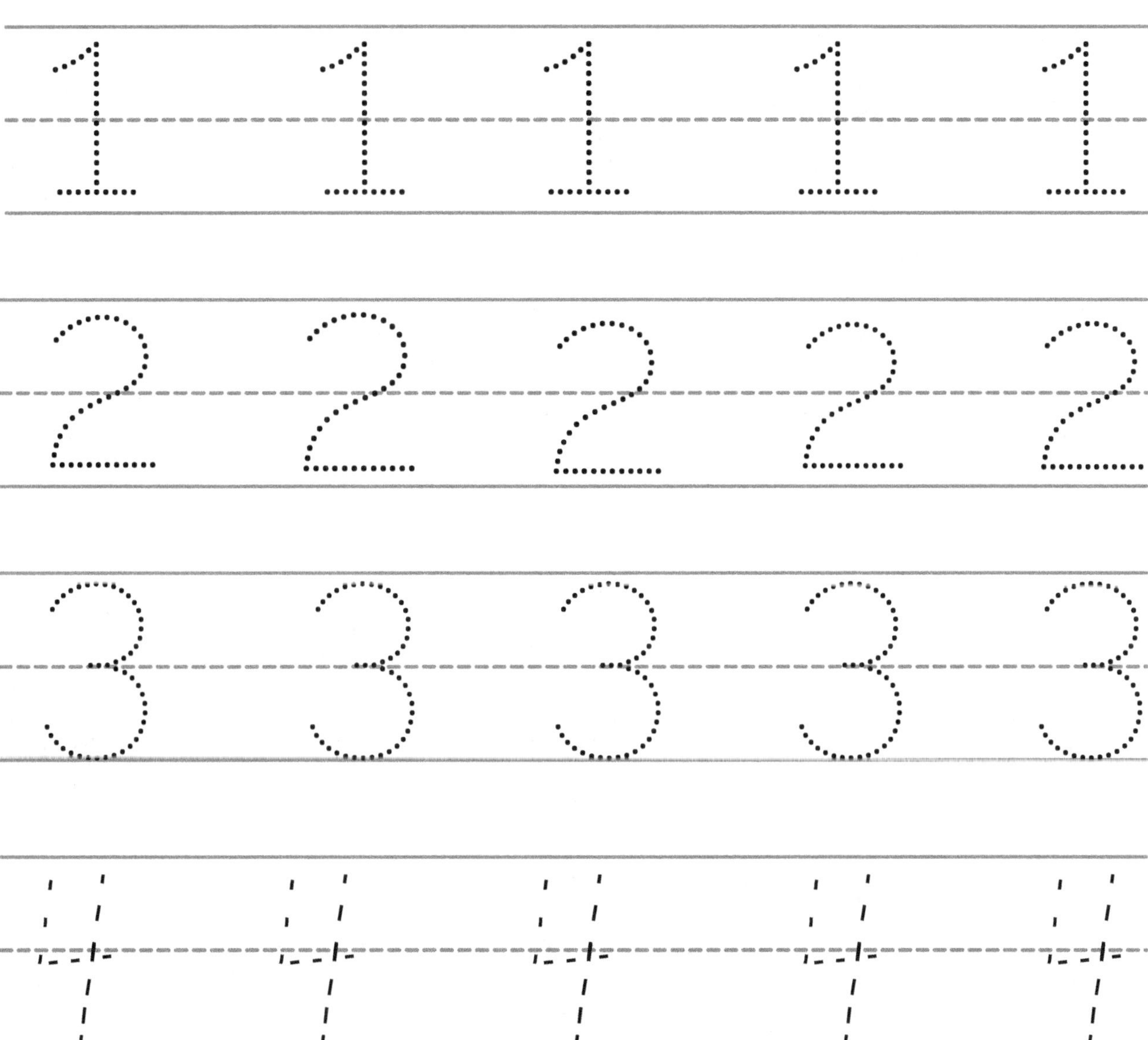

Name _______________________

Trace the numbers from 6 to 10

6 7 8 9 10

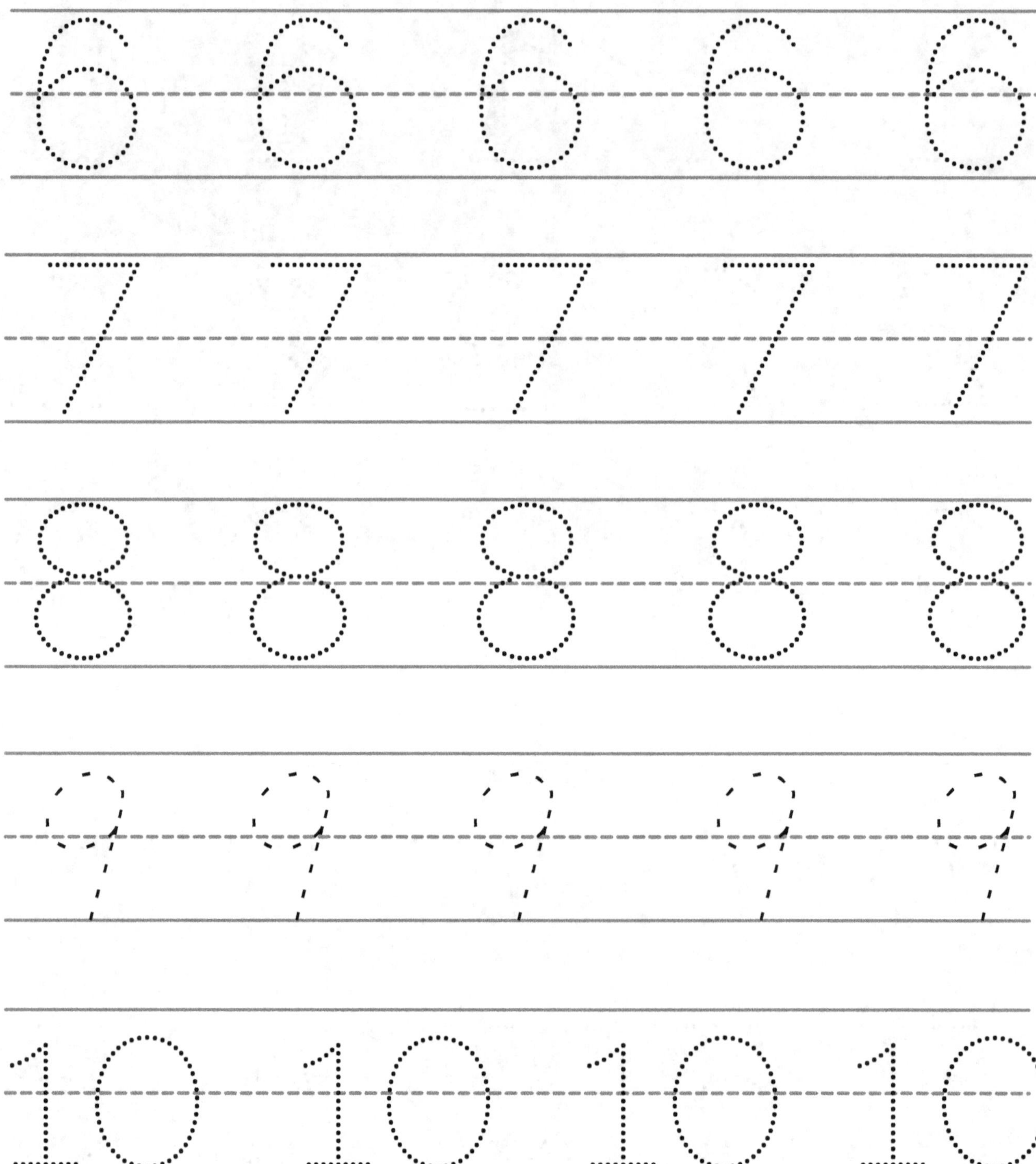

Circle the number that matches the word.

ten   8 10 2

six   6 1 4

one   7 3 1

two   4 7 2

four   9 4 5

Name _______________________

Count and circle the right number for triangles.

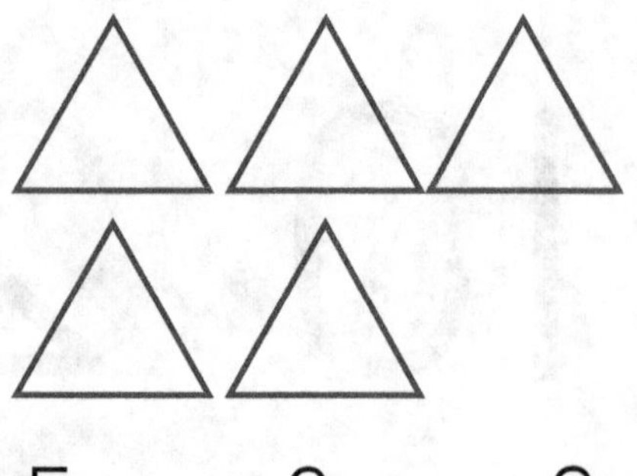

5   2   9

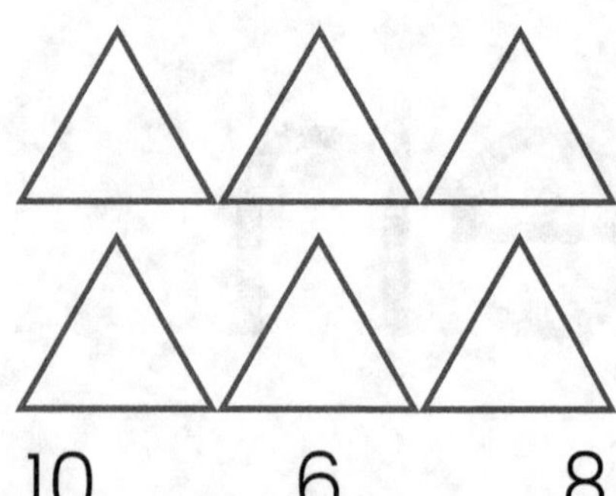

10   6   8

5   3   7

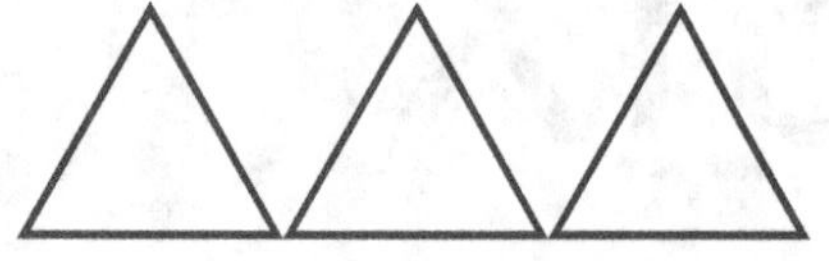

2   3   4

6   9   10

3   4   2

Name

Count and circle the right number for objects.
Trace the number.

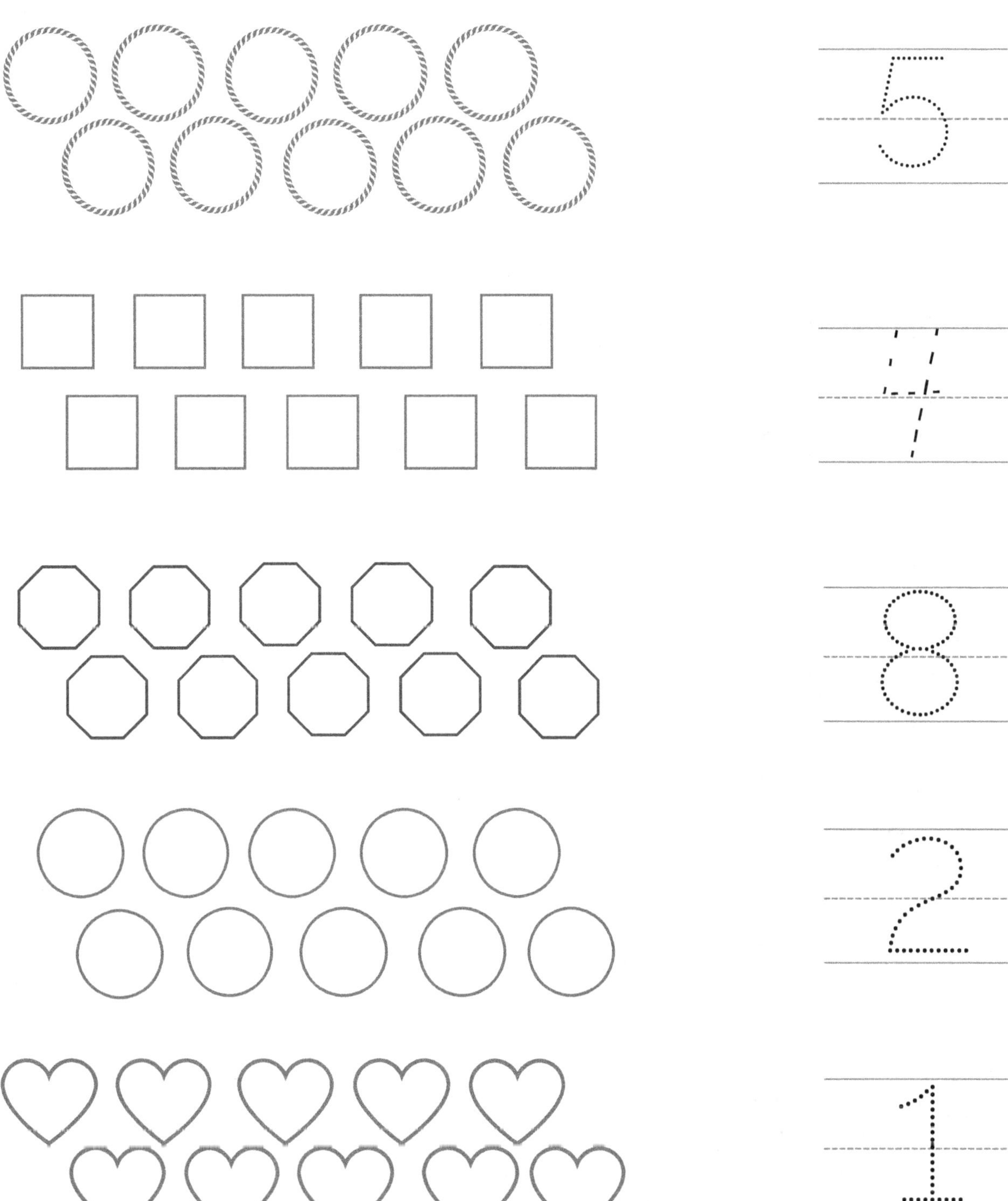

Name

Count and circle the right number for objects.
Trace the number.

Name _______

Draw a line from the object to the match number.

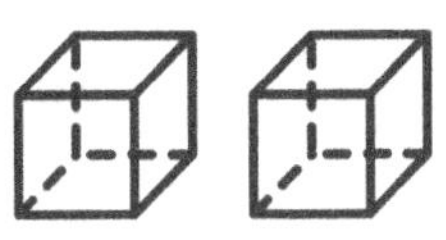

5

9

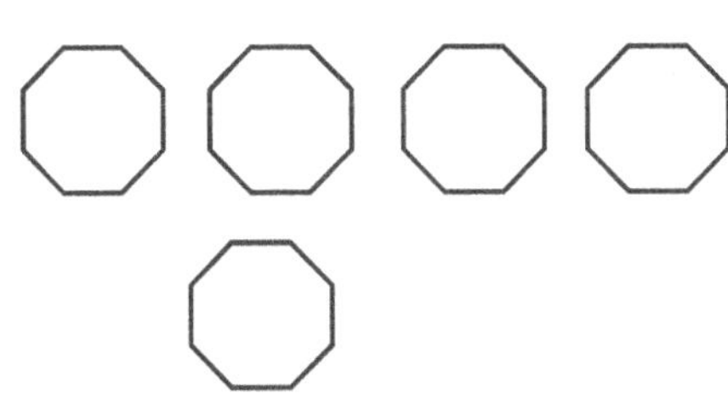

1

2

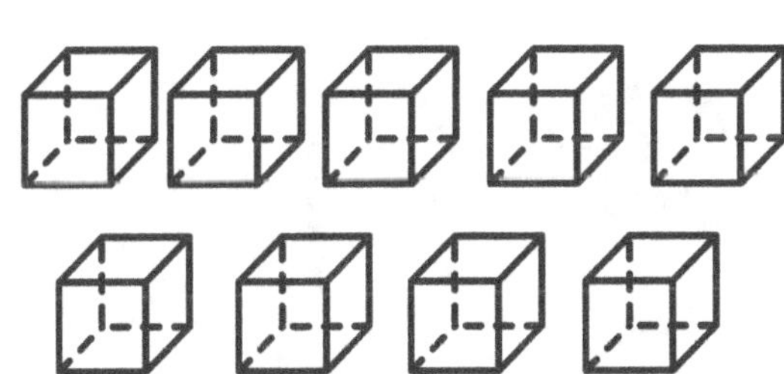

7

Name____________

Fill in the missing number

1 ___ 3   5 ___ 7

2 3 ___   0 ___ 2

8 ___ 10   4 5 ___

___ 5 6   7 ___ 9

6 ___ 8   8 9 ___

Part 2

Practice handwriting with ABCs, matching upper case and lower case letters, fill in the blank, and coloring numbers.

Pages 33-74

Trace the letter A and the word apple.

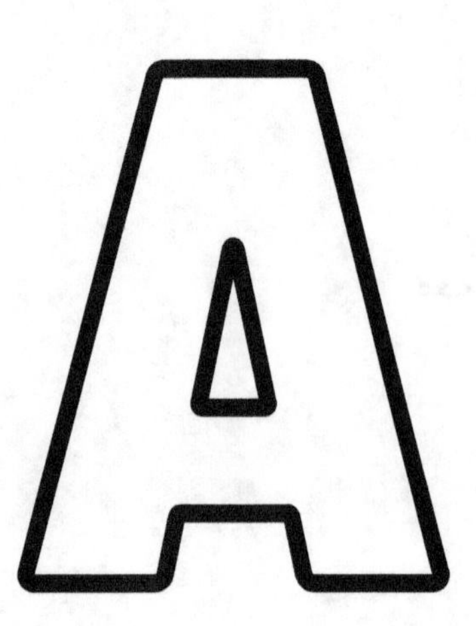

is for apple.

Aa Aa Aa Aa Aa Aa

Aa Aa Aa Aa Aa Aa

apple apple

apple apple

Name

Trace the letter B and the word banana.

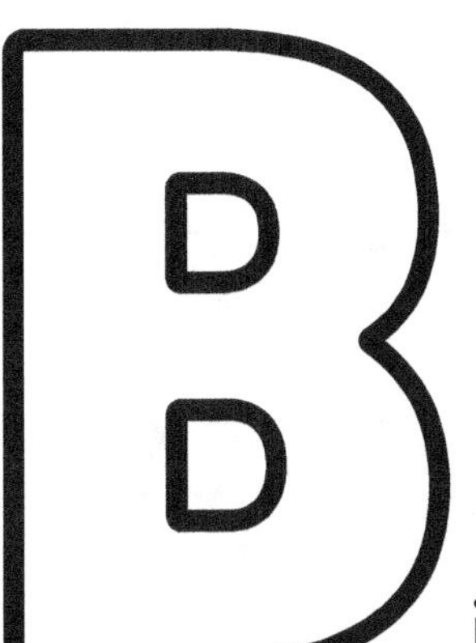

B is for banana.

Bb   Bb   Bb

Bb   Bb   Bb

banana

banana

Name

Trace the letter C and the word car.

is for car.

Name

Trace the letter D and the word dog.

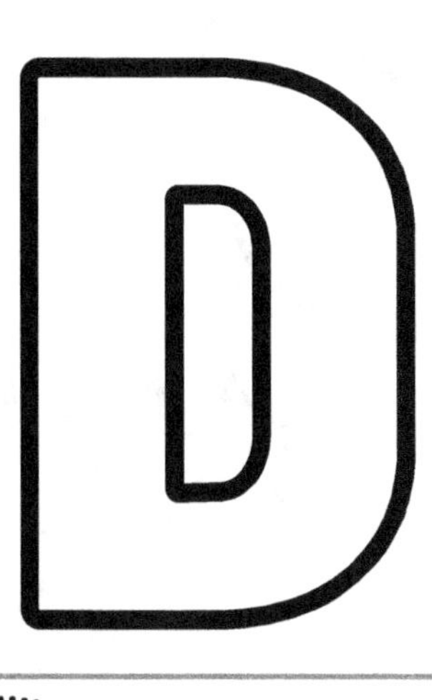

is for dog.

Dd Dd Dd

Dd Dd Dd

dog   dog

dog   dog

Trace the letter E and the word elephant.

E

is for elephant.

Ee Ee Ee Ee

Ee Ee Ee Ee

elephant

elephant

Name

Trace the letter F and the word flower.

is for flower.

Name

Trace the letter G and the word grapes.

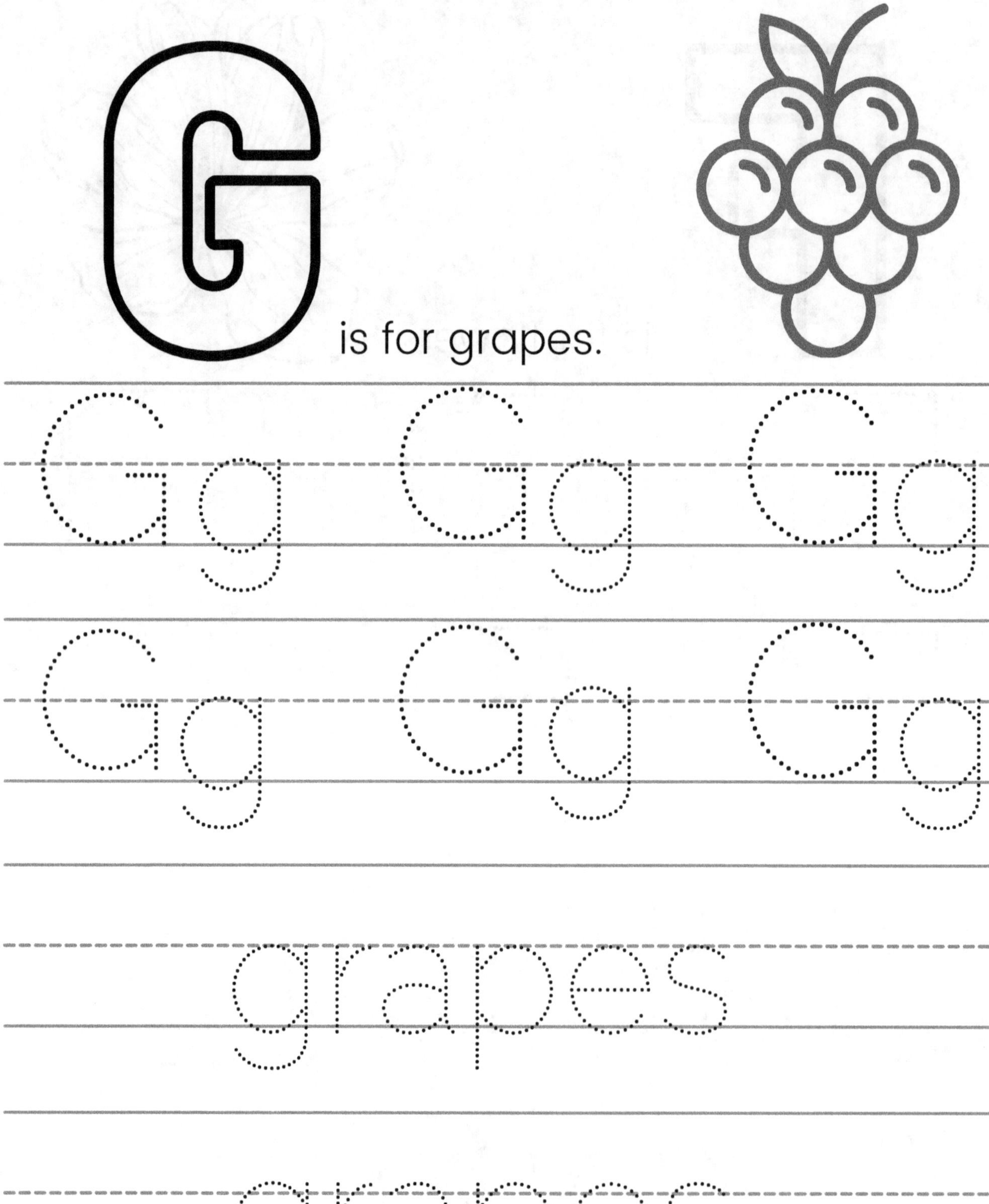

is for grapes.

G g G g G g

G g G g G g

grapes

grapes

Name

Trace the letter H and the word horse.

is for horse.

41

Name

Trace the letter I and the word igloo .

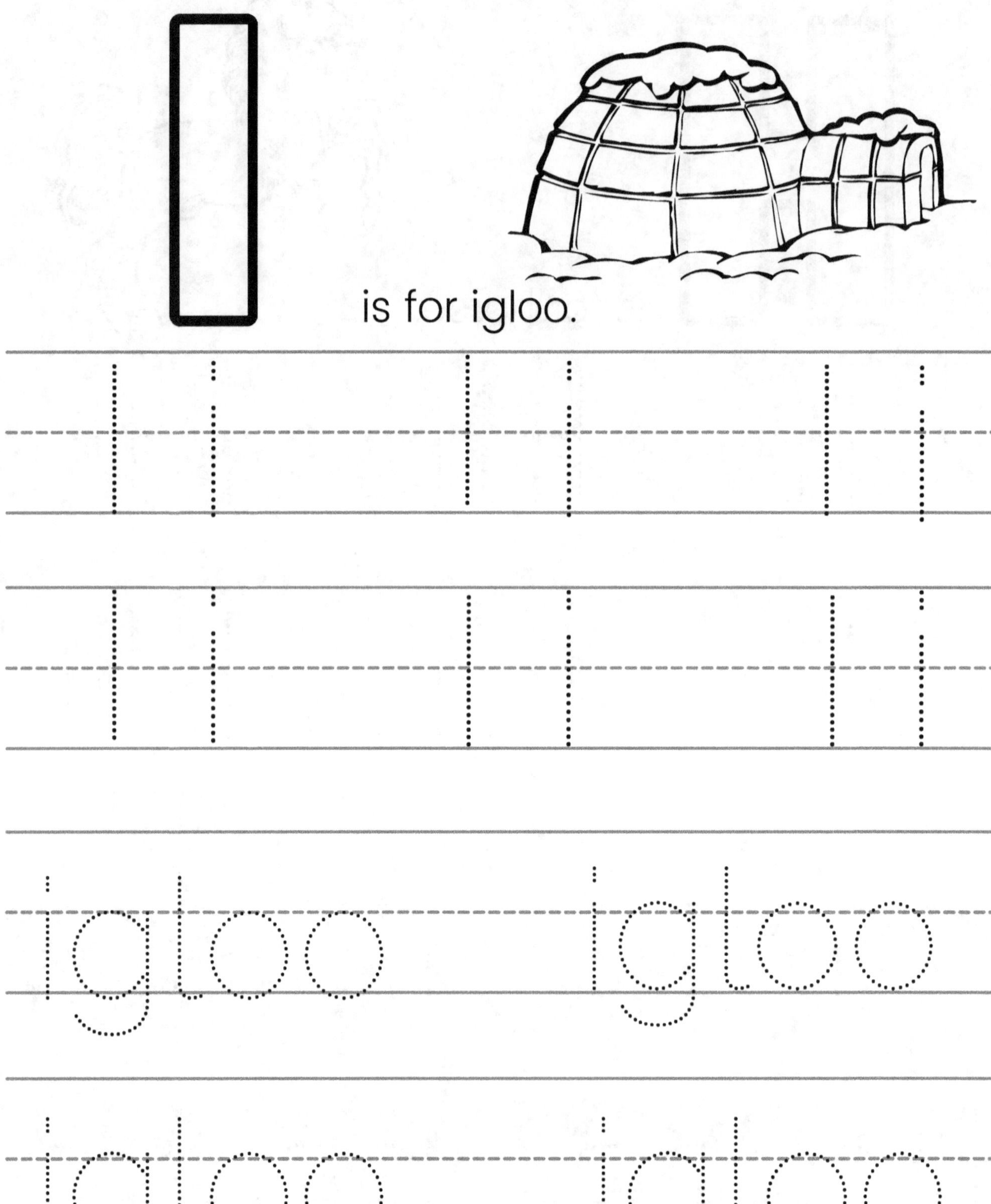

is for igloo.

Name

Trace the letter J and the word jars.

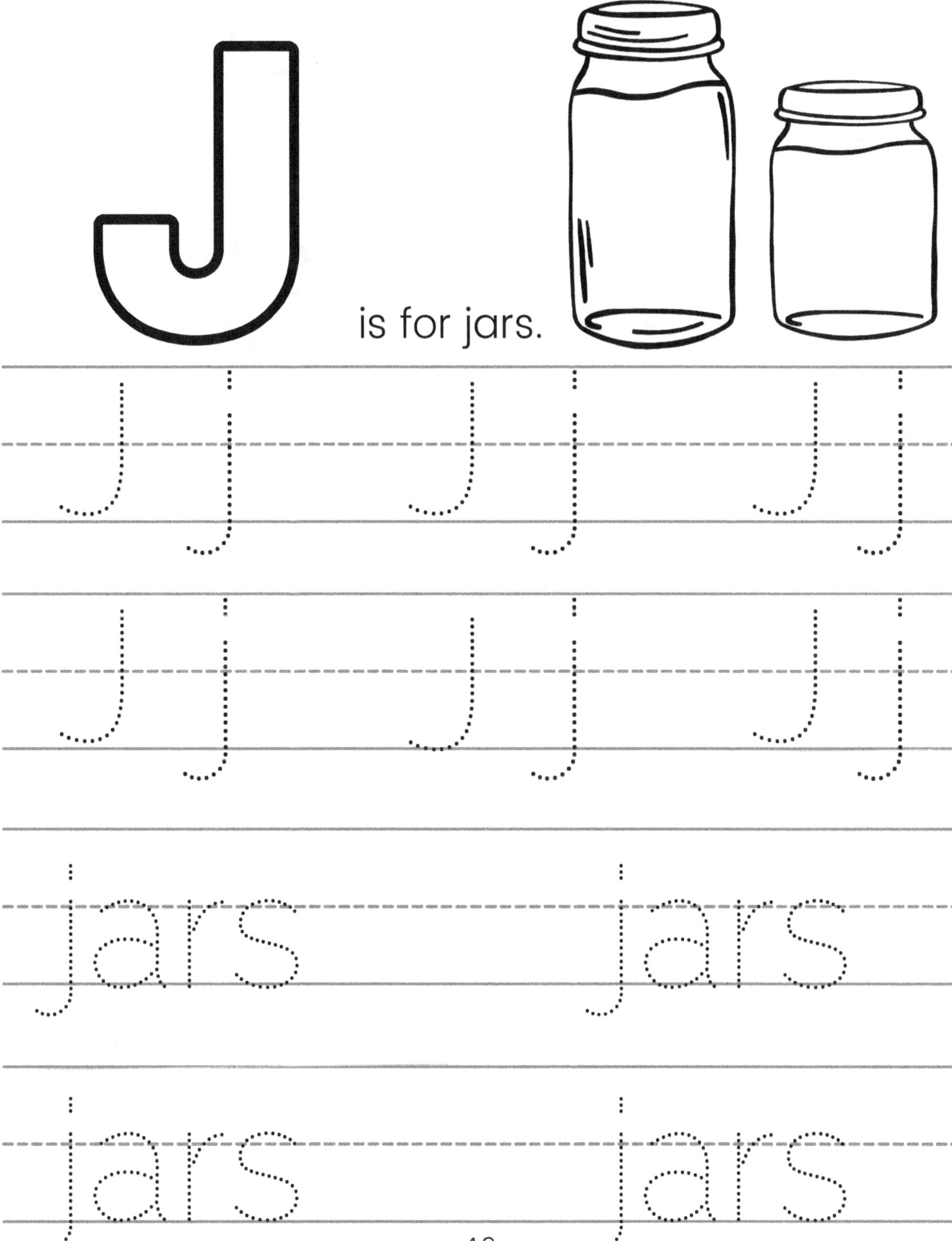

is for jars.

Name______________

Trace the letter K and the word keys.

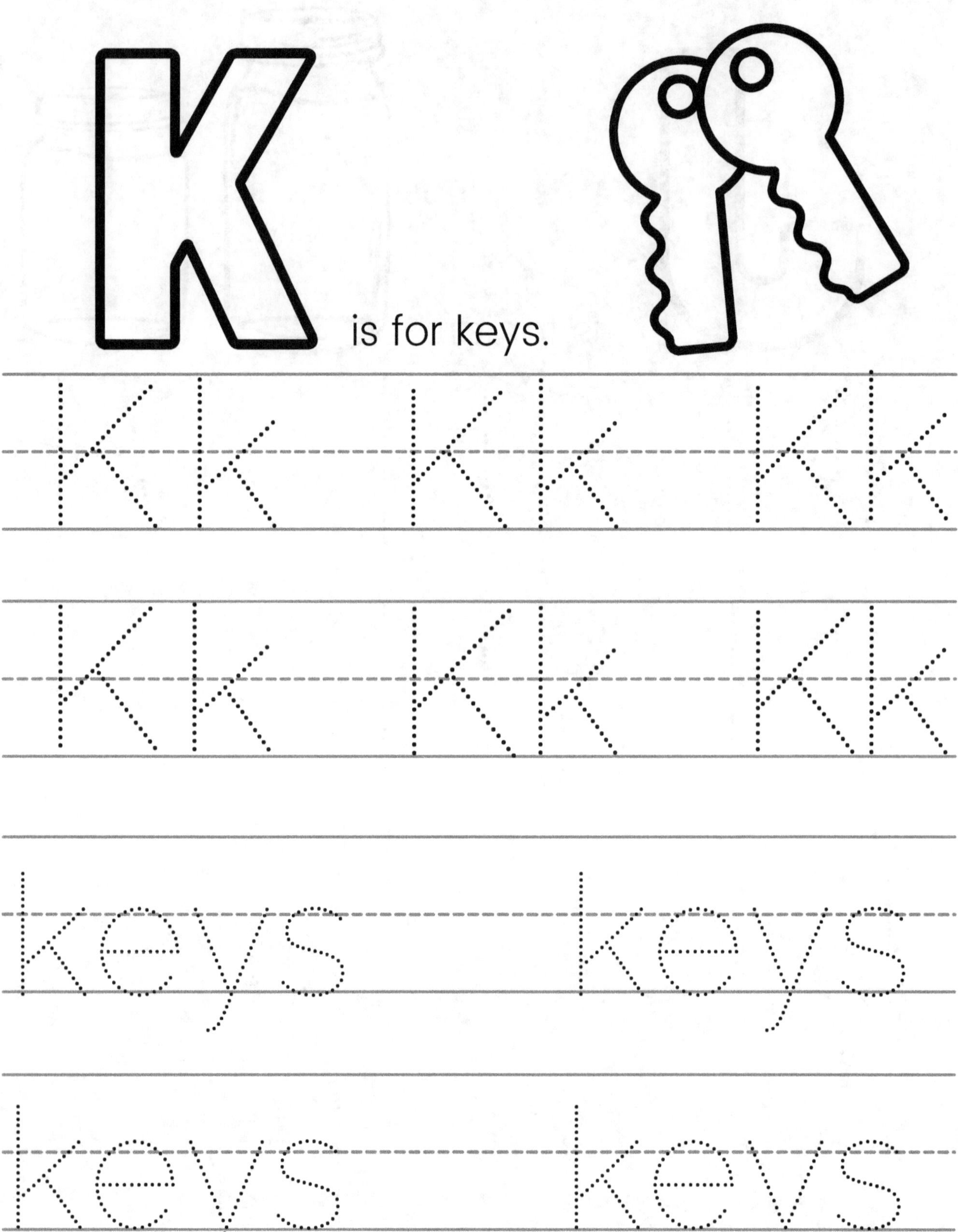

is for keys.

K K K K K K

K K K K K K

keys keys

keys keys

Name

Trace the letter L and the word leaves.

L

is for leaves.

leaves

leaves

Name

Trace the letter M and the word milk.

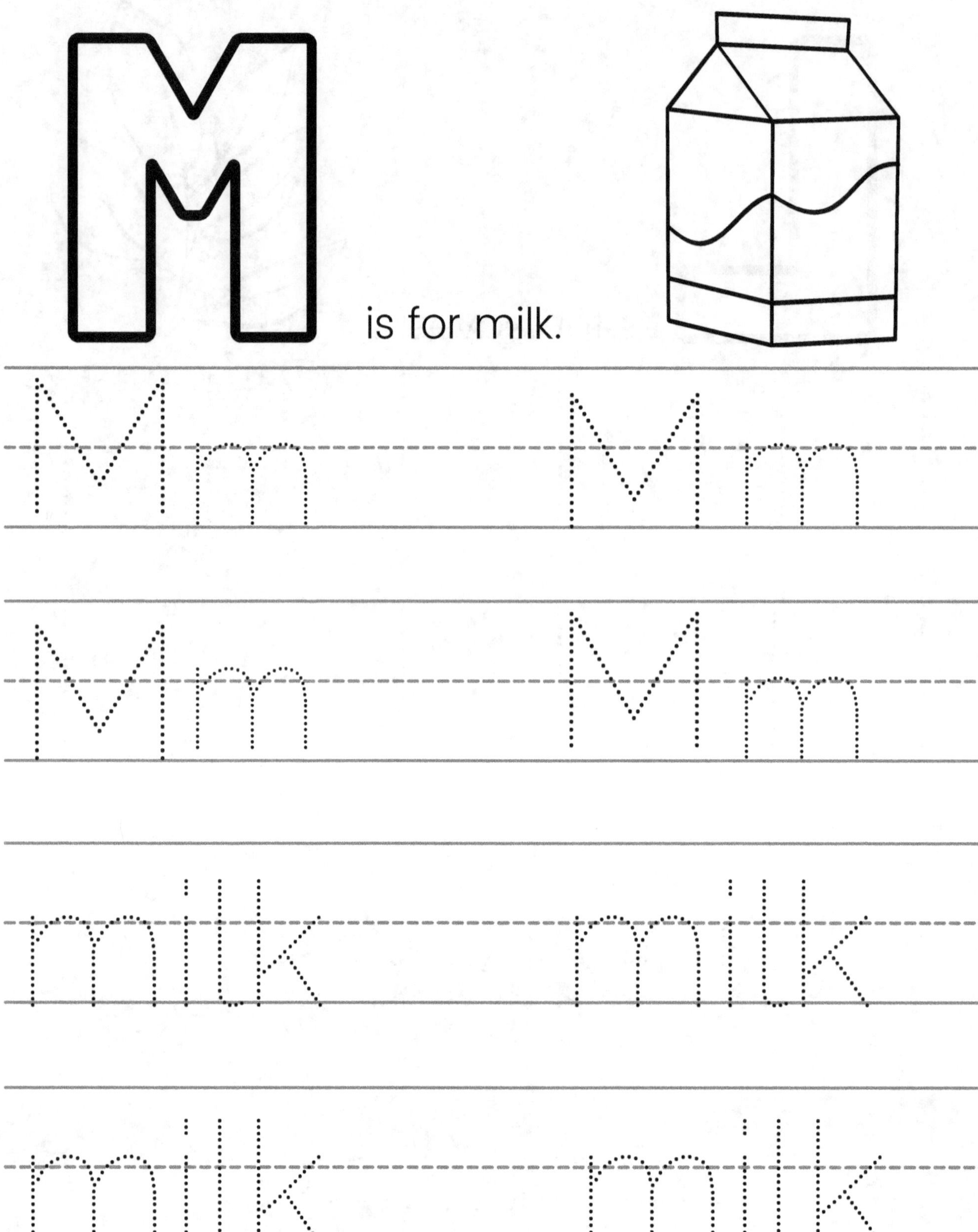

is for milk.

46

Trace the letter N and the word nest.

N

is for nest.

Nn Nn Nn

Nn Nn Nn

nest   nest

nest   nest

Name

Trace the letter O and the word orange.

is for orange.

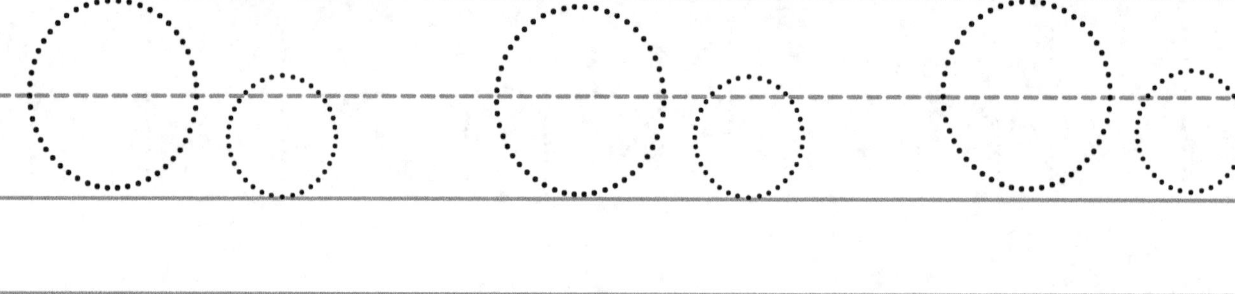

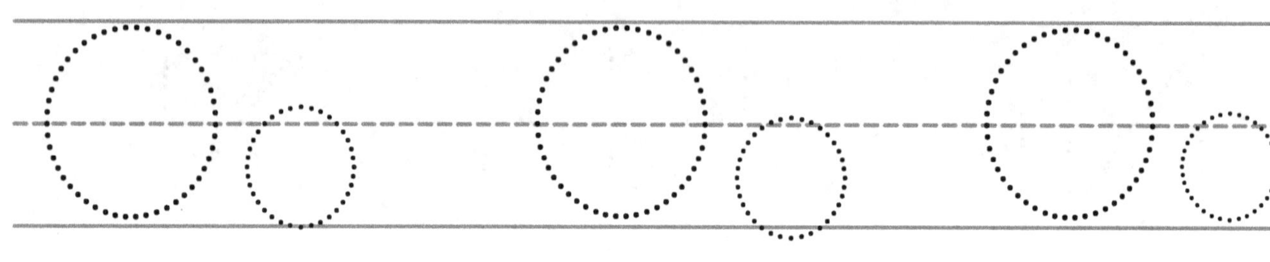

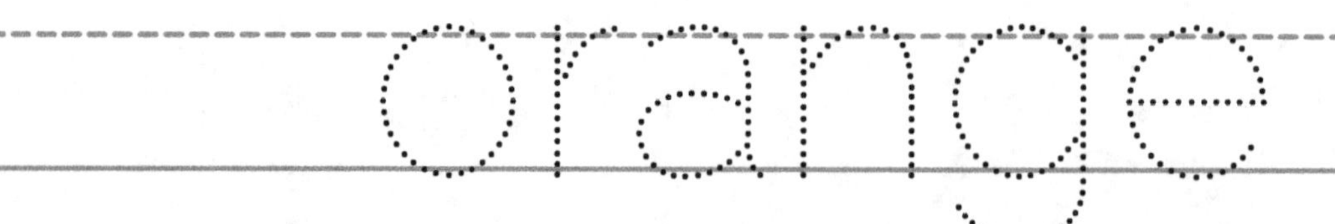

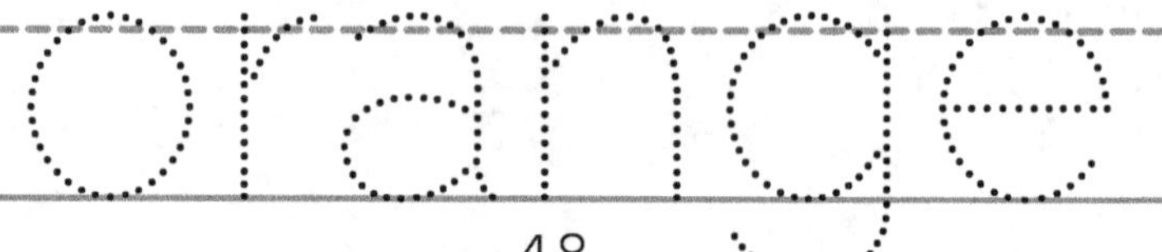

Name____________________

Trace the letter P and the word pear.

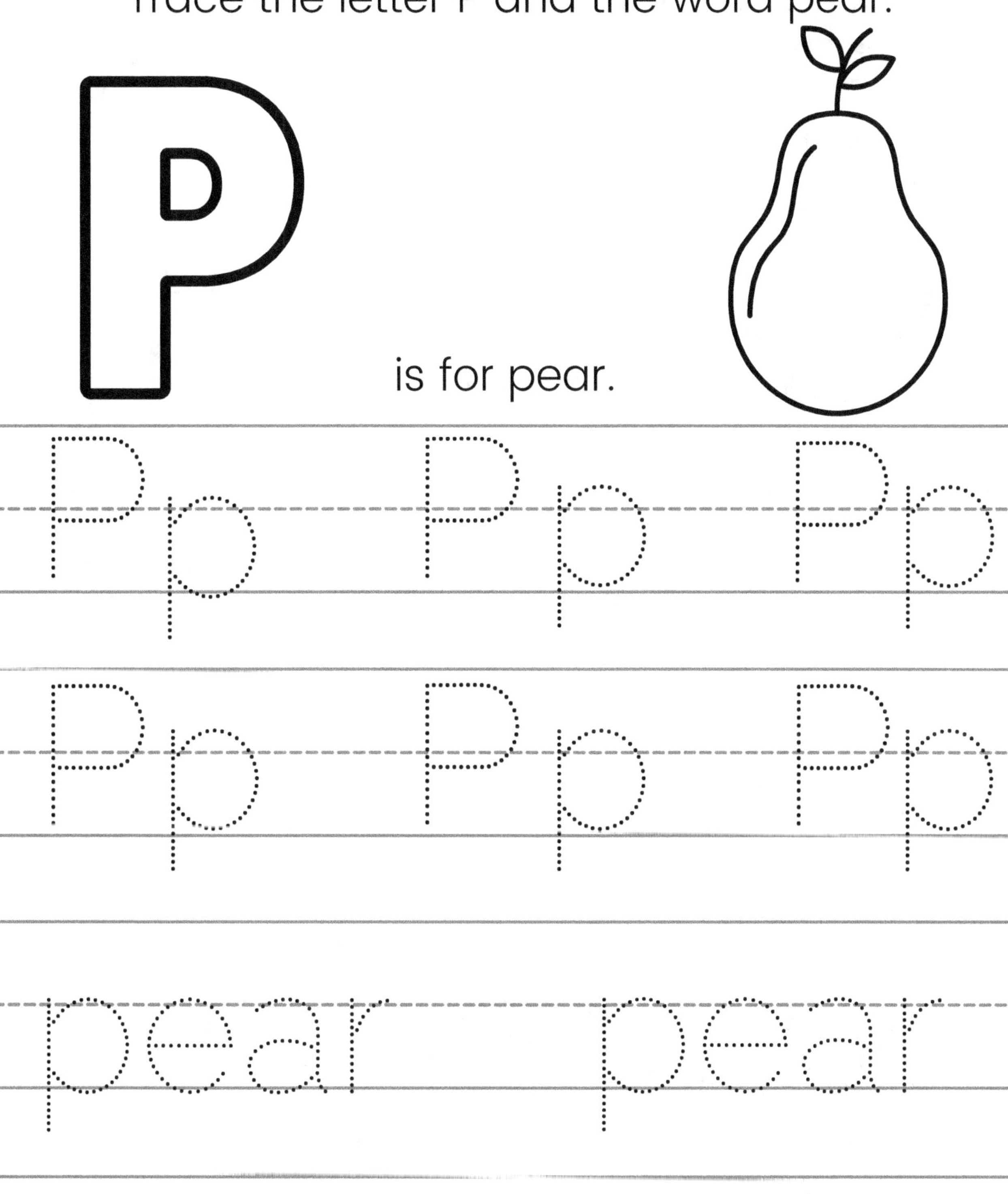

is for pear.

P p   P p   P p

P p   P p   P p

pear   pear

pear   pear

Name

Trace the letter Q and the word question.

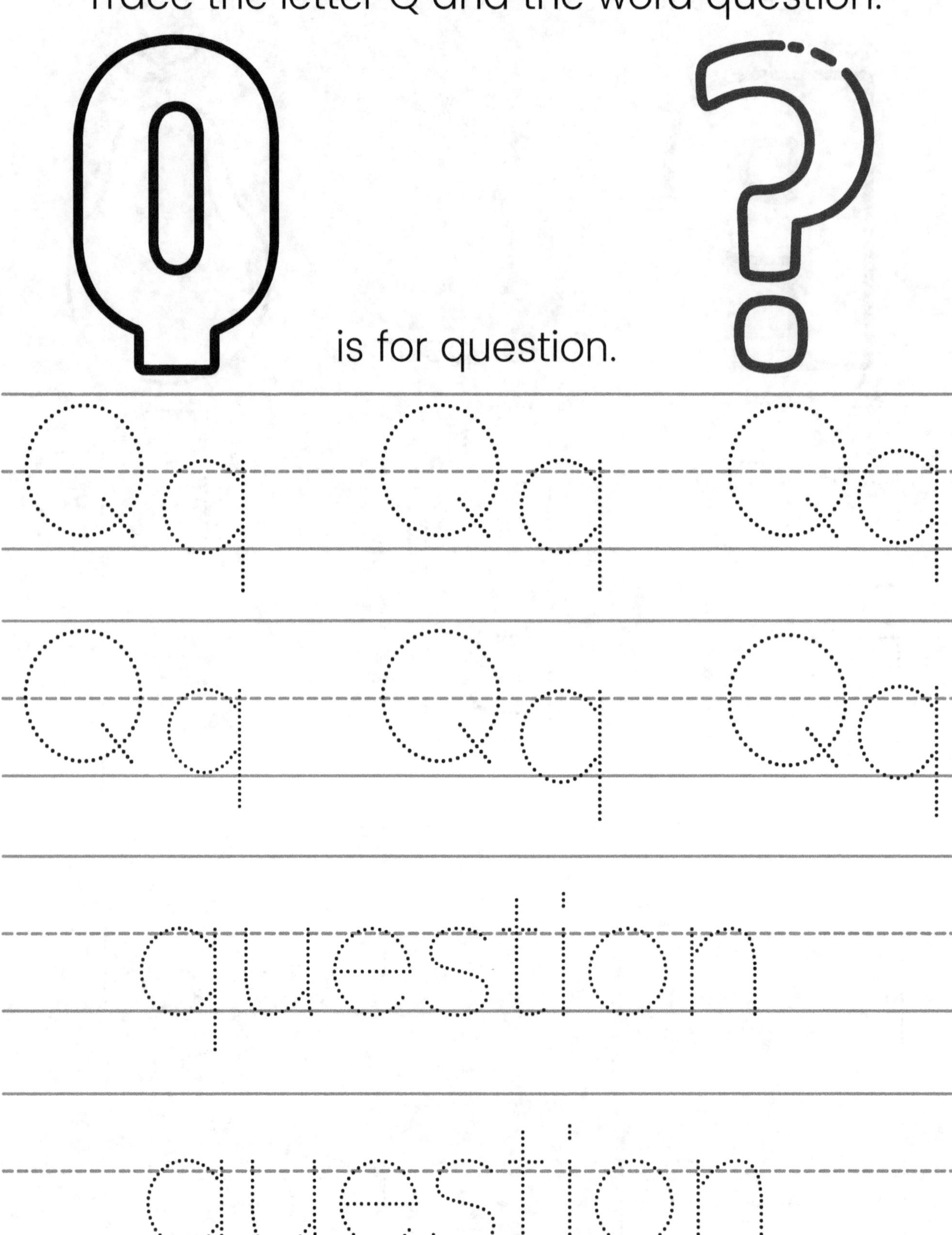

is for question.

Name ____________________

Trace the letter R and the word rose.

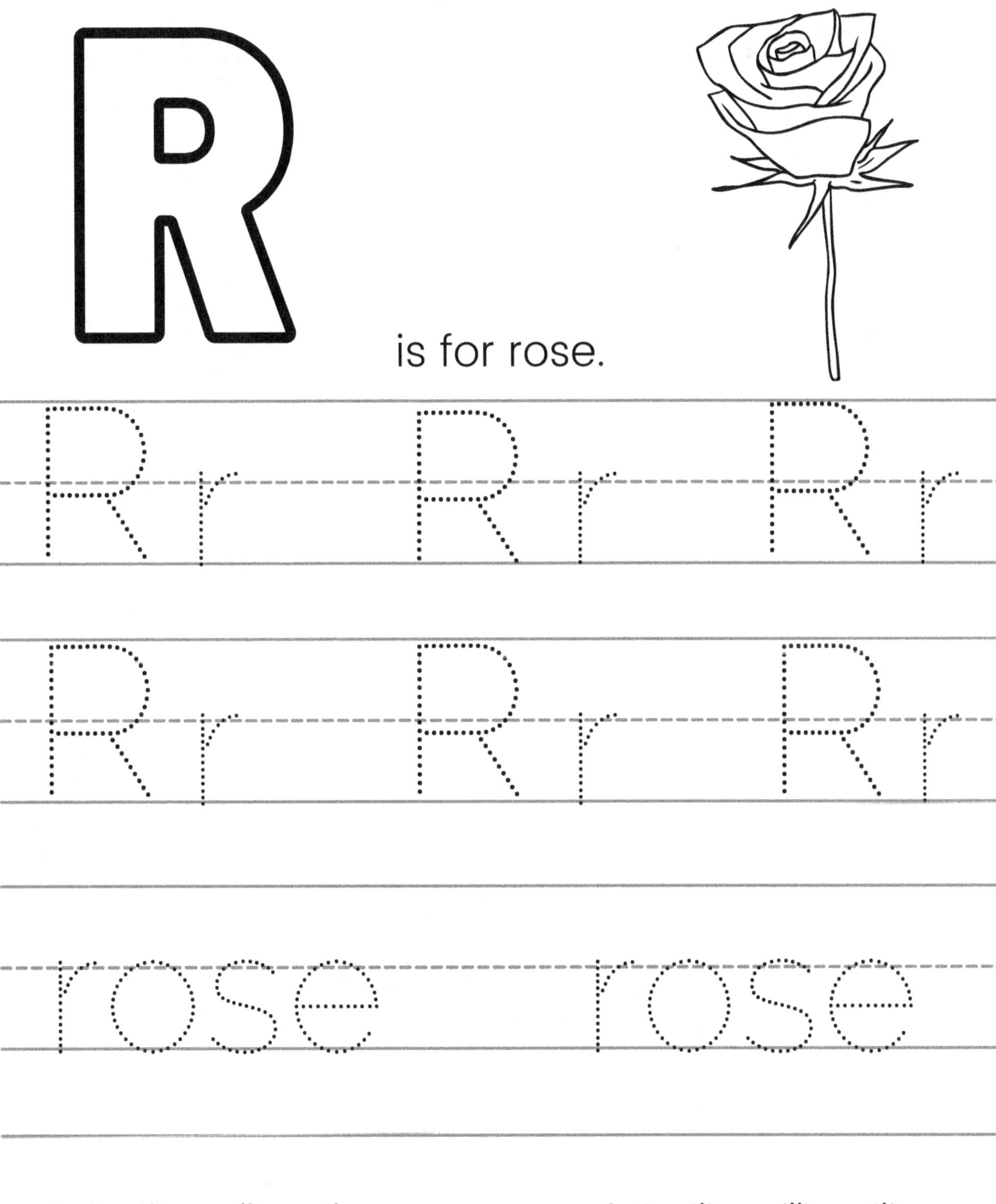

is for rose.

Name_______________

Trace the letter S and the word strawberry.

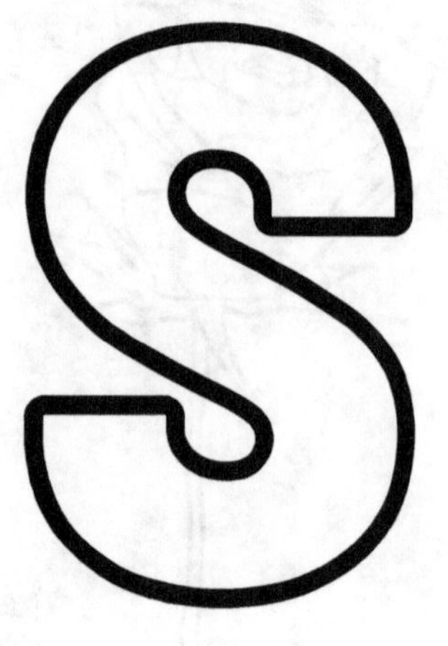

is for strawberry.

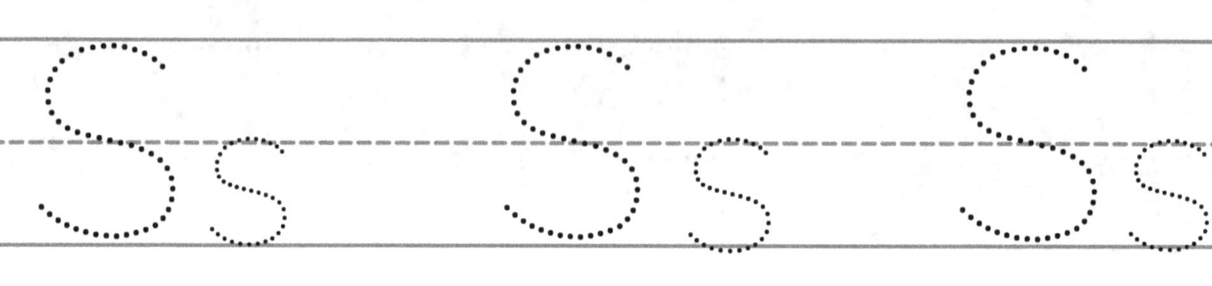

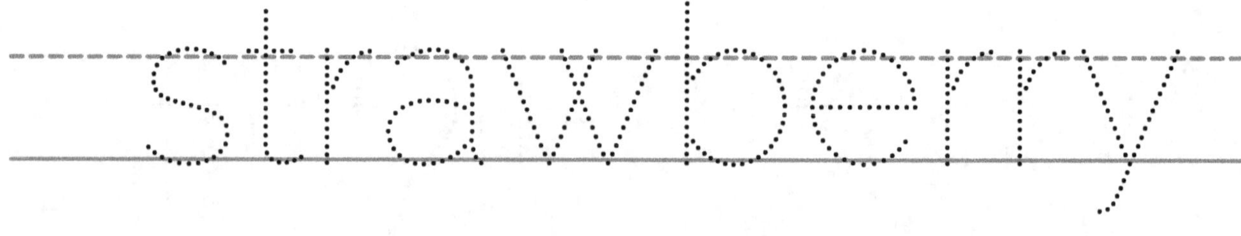

Name _______________

Trace the letter T and the word turtle.

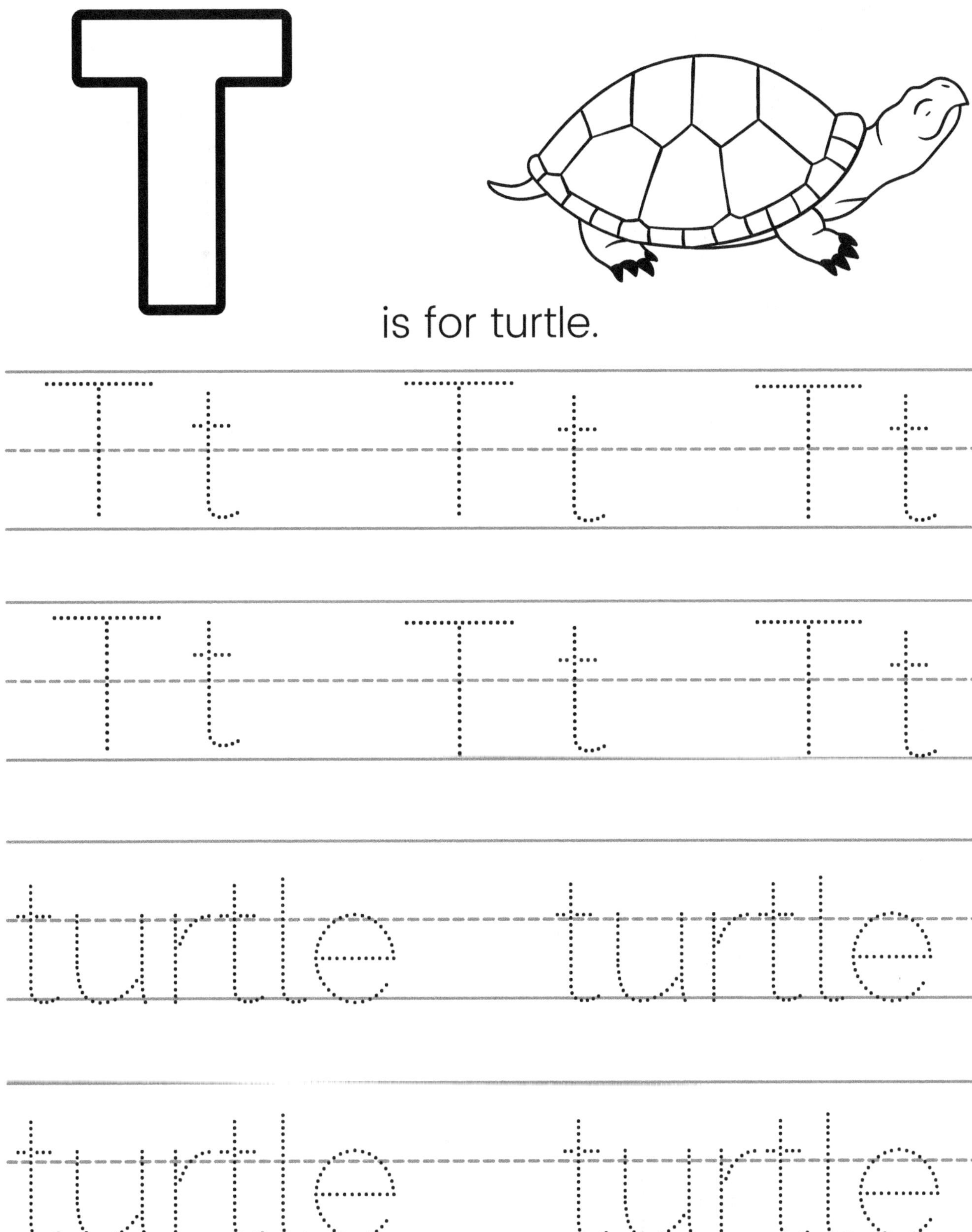

is for turtle.

T t   T t   T t

T t   T t   T t

turtle   turtle

turtle   turtle

Name

Trace the letter U and the word umbrella.

is for umbrella.

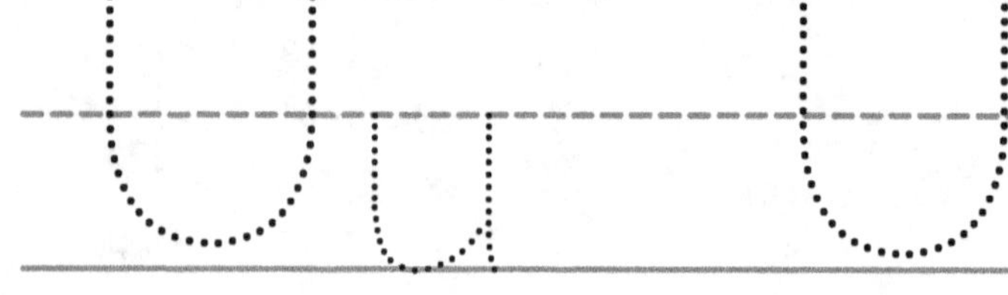

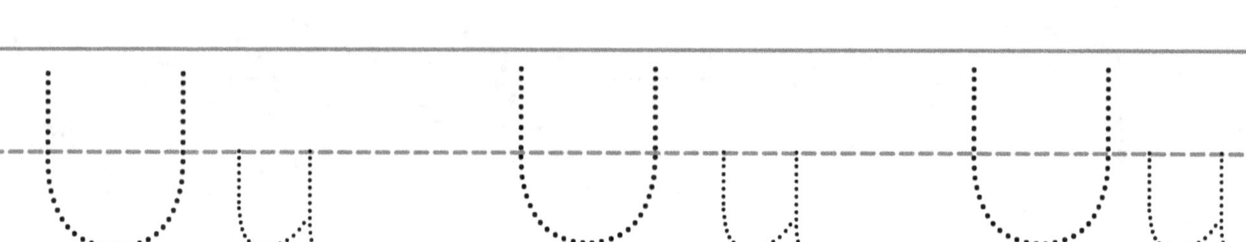

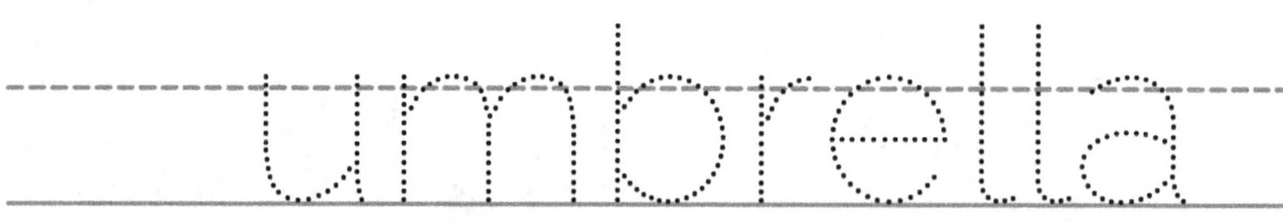

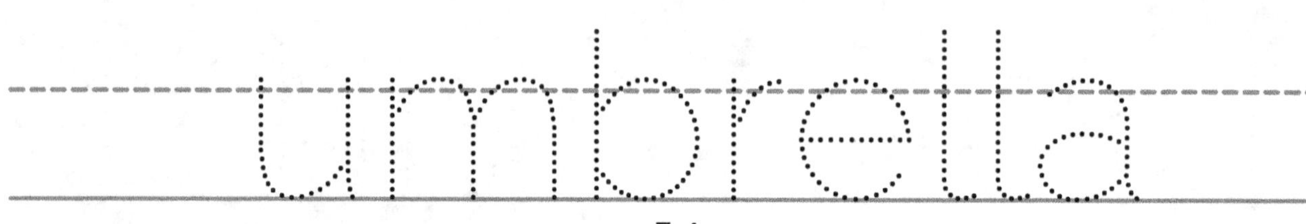

Name

Trace the letter V and the word vase.

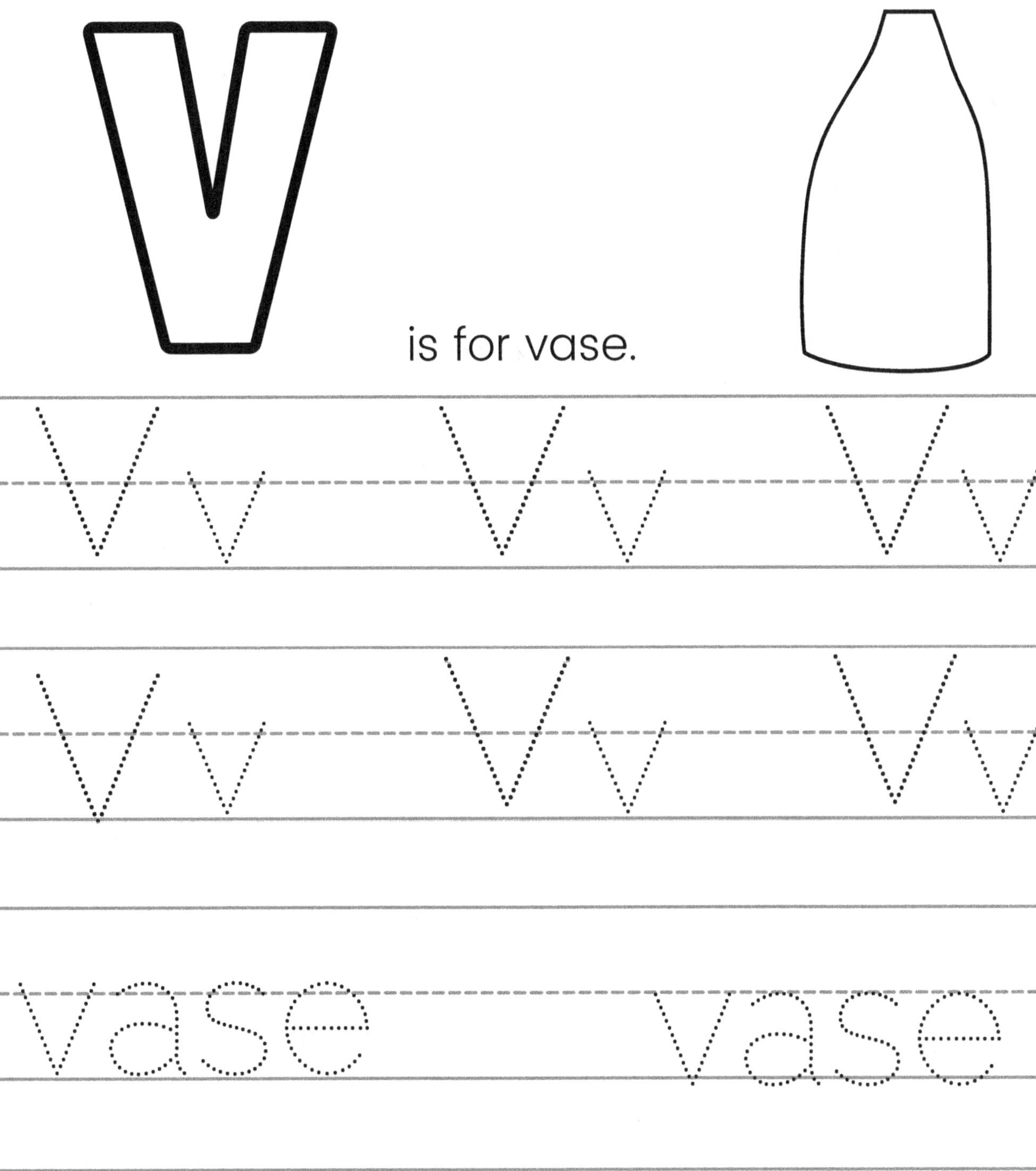

is for vase.

Name

Trace the letter W and the word watermelon .

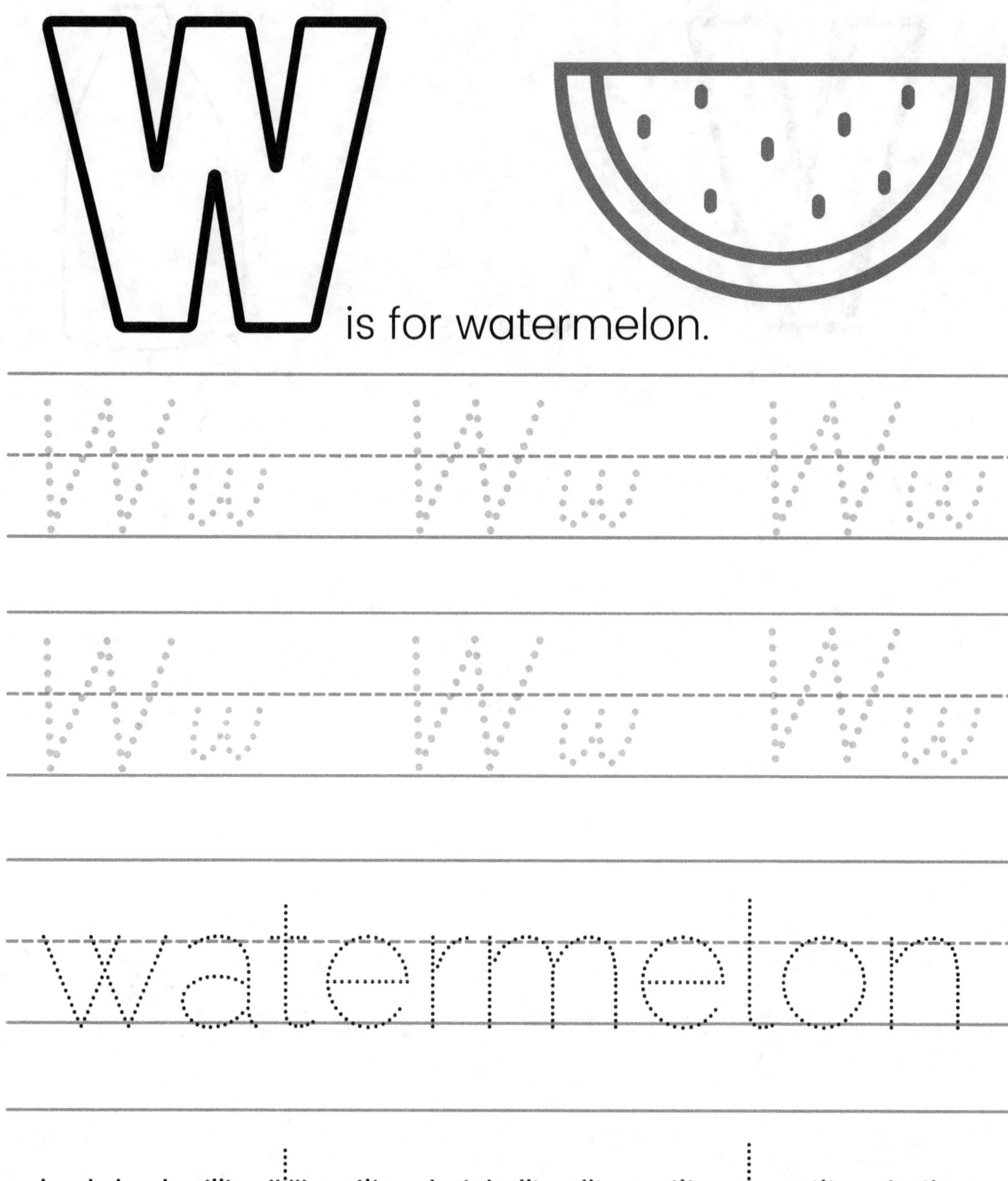

W is for watermelon.

w w w w w w

W W W W W W

watermelon

watermelon

Name

Trace the letter X and the word xylophone.

is for xylophone.

Name

Trace the letter Y and the word yarn.

is for yarn.

Y Y Y Y Y Y

Y Y Y Y Y Y

yarn   yarn

yarn   yarn

Name

Trace the letter Z and the word zebra.

Z

is for zebra.

Z Z Z Z Z Z

Z Z Z Z Z Z

zebra   zebra

zebra   zebra

Name

Practice tracing and writing uppercase ABC letters.

A B C D E

A A

B B

C C

D D

E E

Name

Practice tracing and writing uppercase ABC letters.

F G H I J

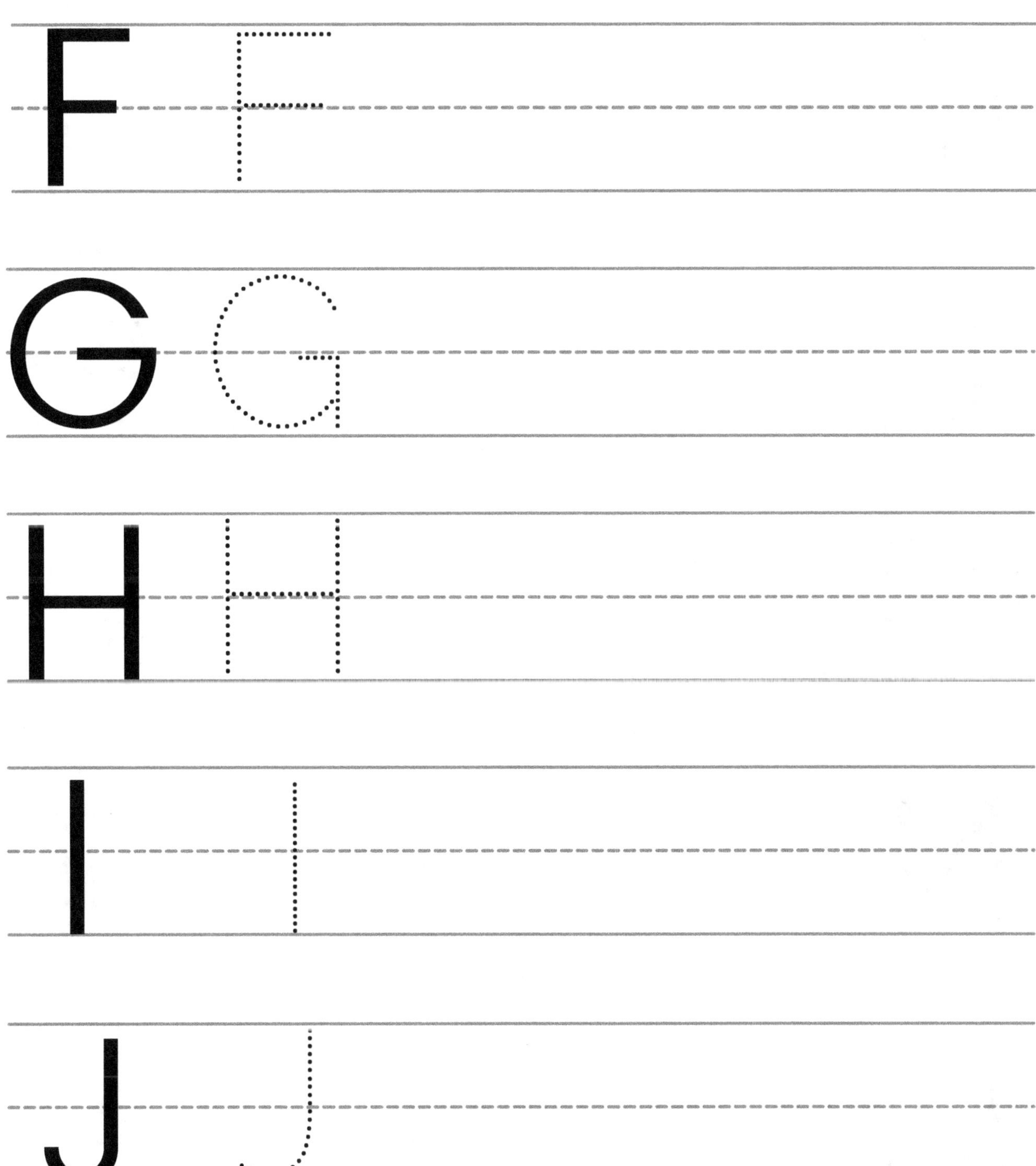

Name _______________

Practice tracing and writing uppercase ABC letters.

K L M N O

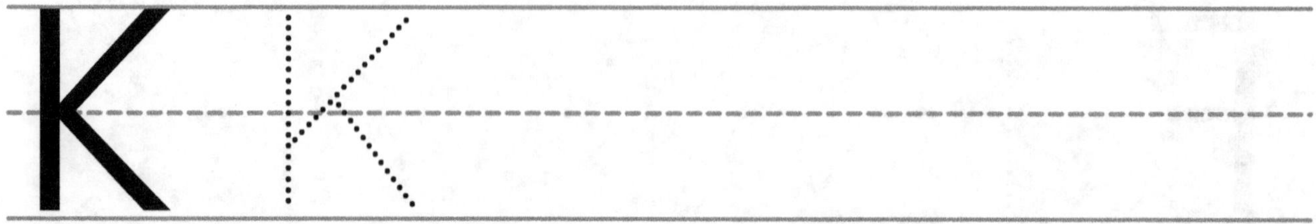

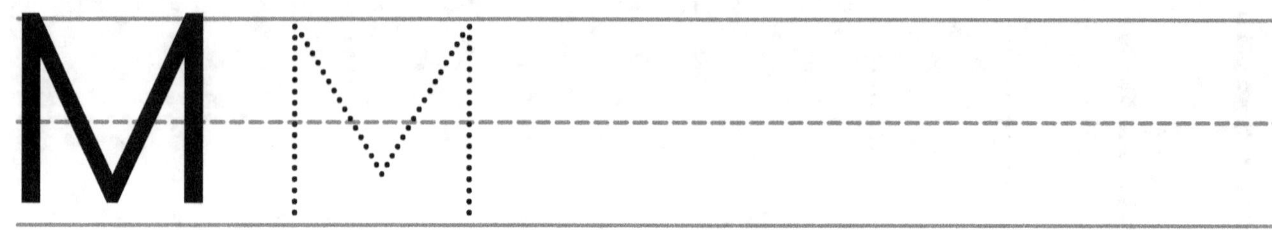

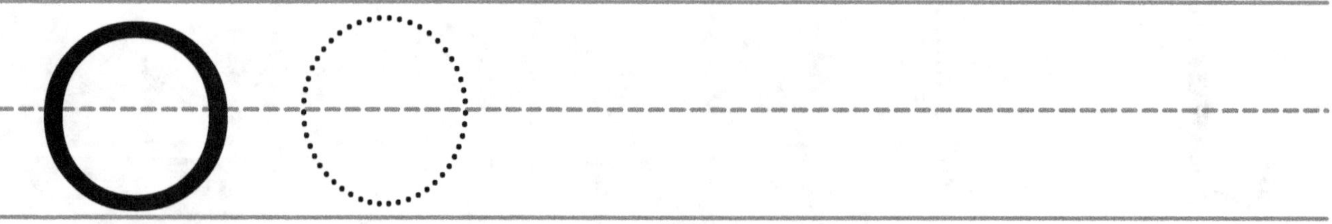

Name

Practice tracing and writing uppercase ABC letters.

P   Q   R   S   T

P P

Q Q

R R

S S

T T

Name

Practice tracing and writing uppercase ABC letters.

U V W X Y

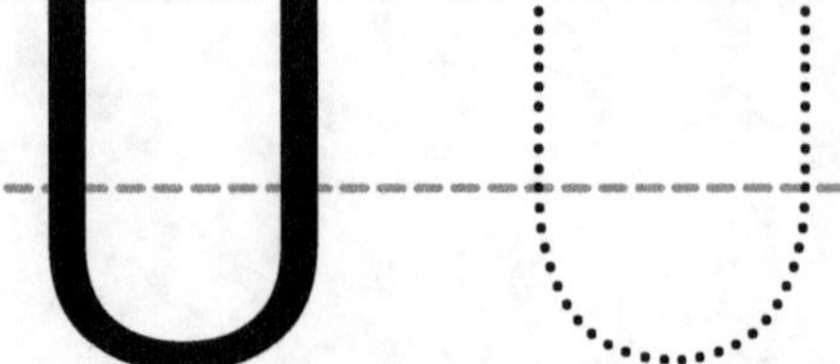

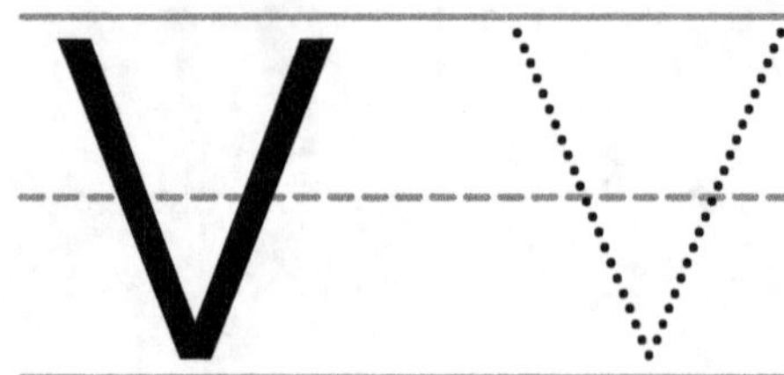

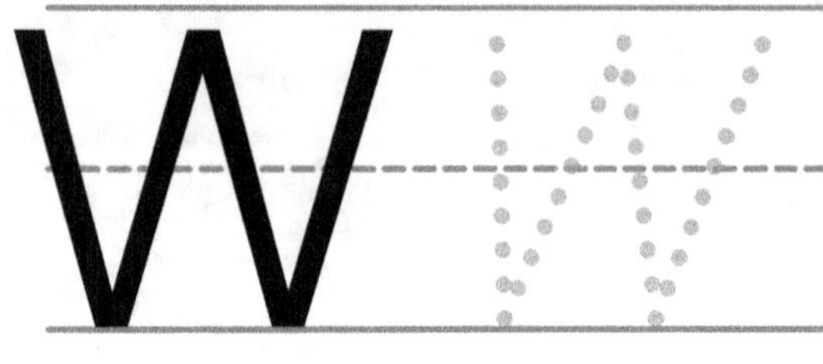

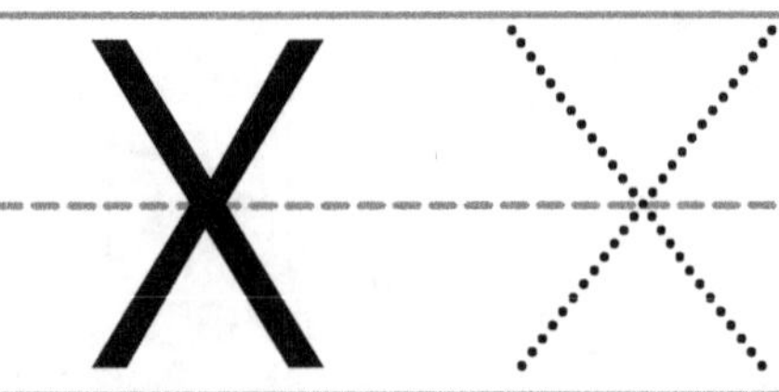

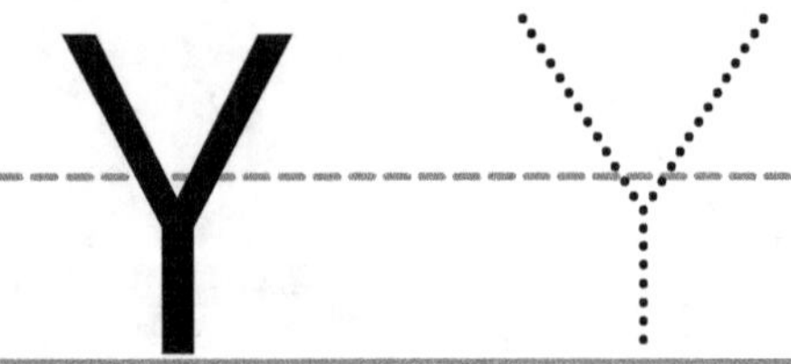

Name _____________

Practice tracing and writing uppercase and lower case ABC letters.

Z a b c d

Z Z

a a

b b

c c

d d

Name ___________

Practice tracing and writing uppercase and lower case ABC letters.

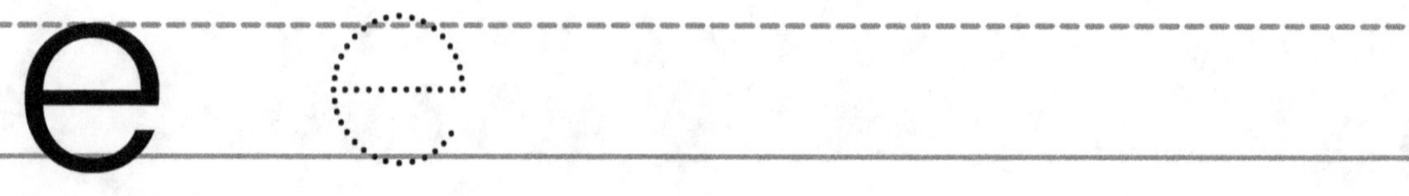

e f g h i

e

f

g

h

i

Name

Practice tracing and writing uppercase and lower case ABC letters.

j   k   l   m   n

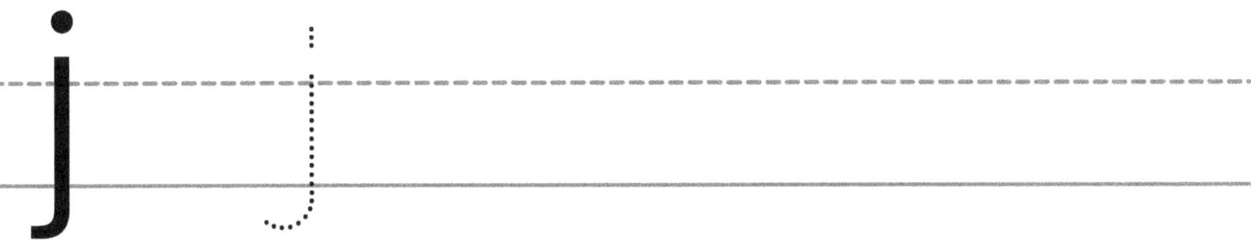

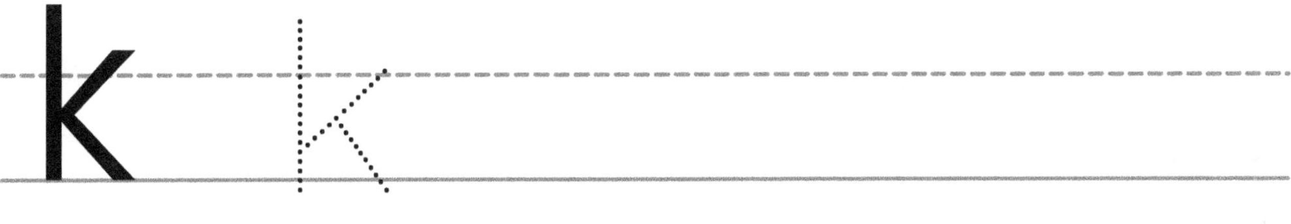

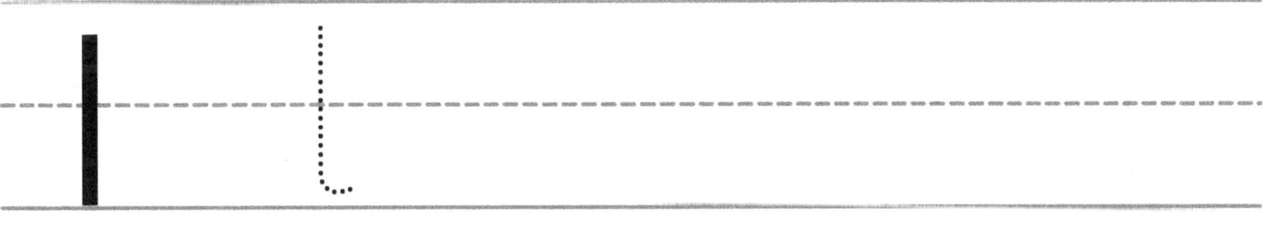

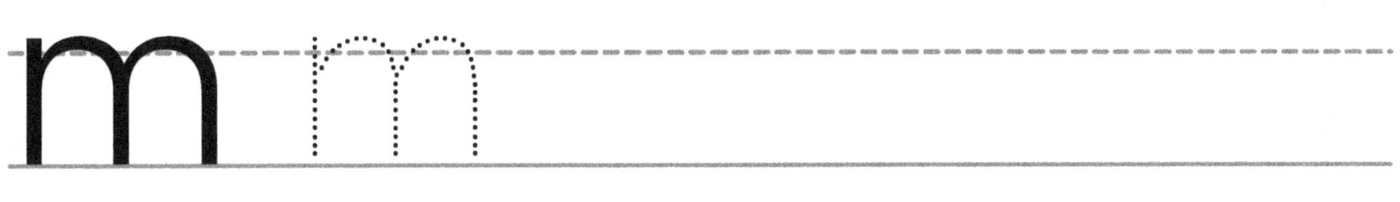

Name

Practice tracing and writing uppercase and
lower case ABC letters.

o p q r s

o

p

q

r

s

Name

Practice tracing and writing uppercase and lower case ABC letters.

t u v w x

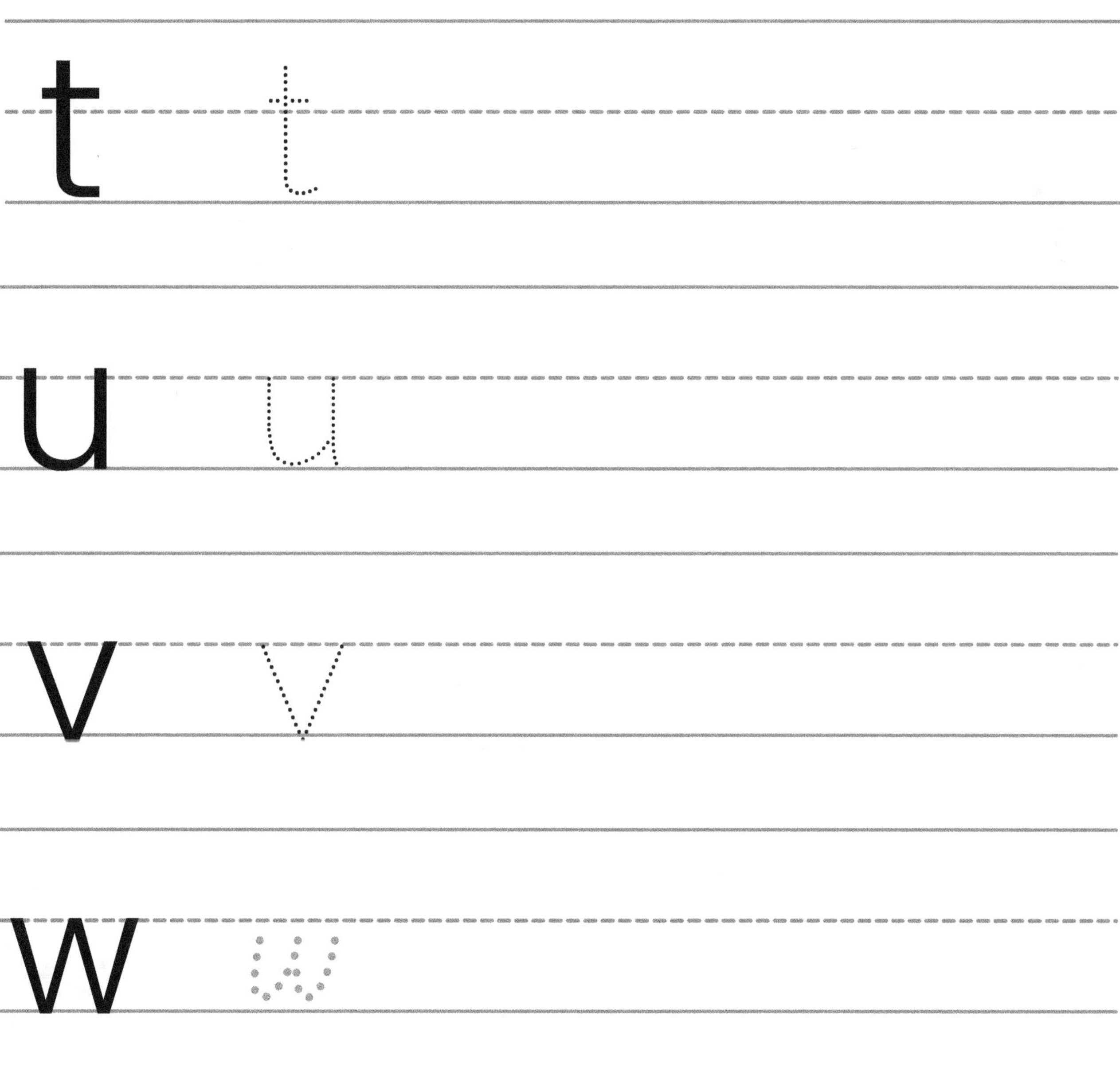

Name

Practice tracing and writing uppercase and
lower case ABC letters.
y z

y y

z z

Match uppercase letters with lower case letters.

H

Q

S

T

C

I

A

i

s

a

q

t

h

c

Match uppercase letters with lower case letters.

U

E

F

T

Q

Y

Z

y

t

z

q

f

e

U

Name

Trace and fill in the matching letter

D S e

z c a

P Y U

d H i

t B o

Name _______________

Fill in the missing alphabet

C _______ E   _______ E F

U V _______   I J _______

K _______ M   X _______ Z

_______ M N   A B _______

N O _______   _______ R S

Part 3

Practice and learn addition and subtraction for toddlers.

Pages 75-85

Name____________________

Addition: Fill in the blank.

$2 + 2 =$ ____________

$3 + 4 =$ ____________

$1 + 2 =$ ____________

Name________________

Addition: Fill in the blank.

6+2 = ________

3+3 = ________

2+5 = ________

Name

Addition: Fill in the blank.

Addition: Fill in the blank.

3 + 0 = _______

5 + 4 = _______

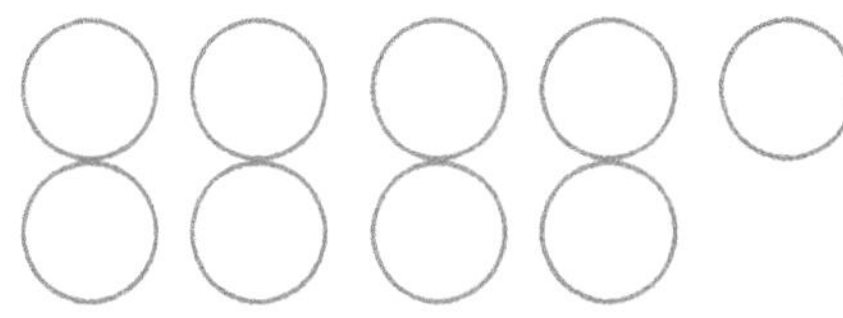

0 + 2 = _______

Name _______________

Addition: Fill in the blank.

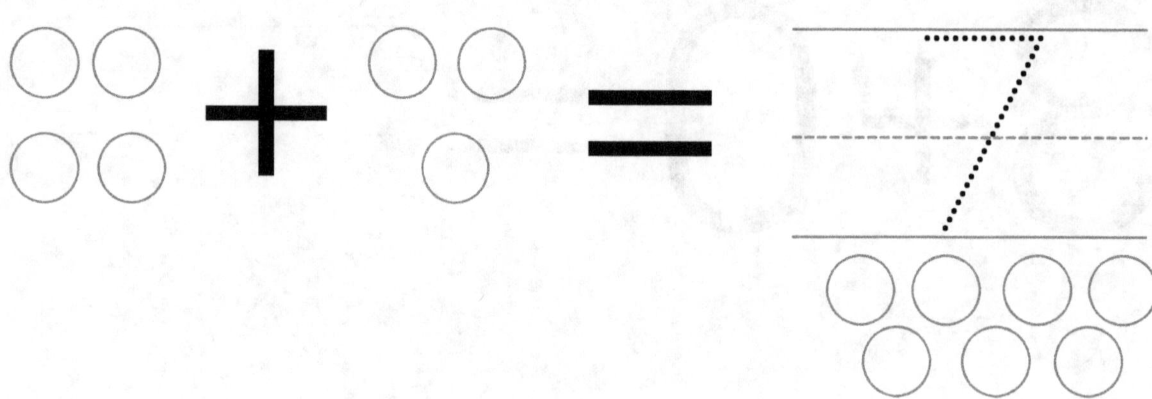

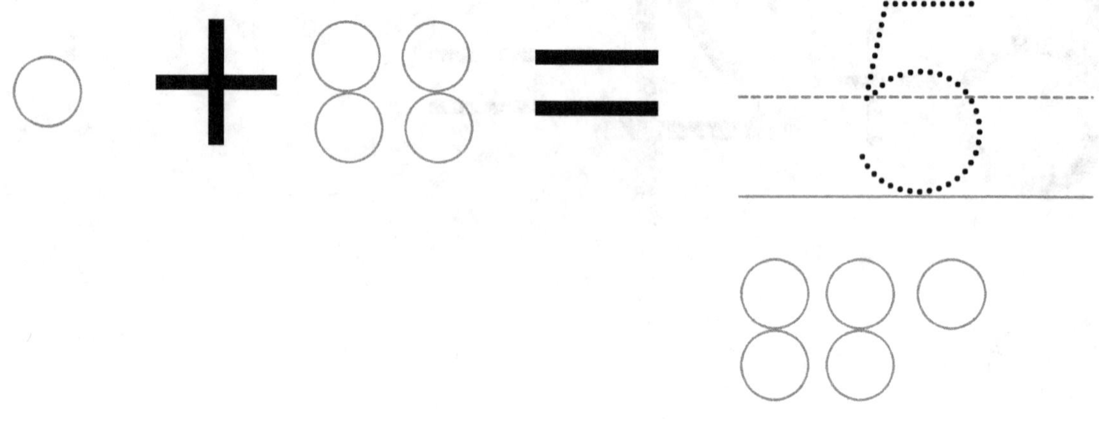

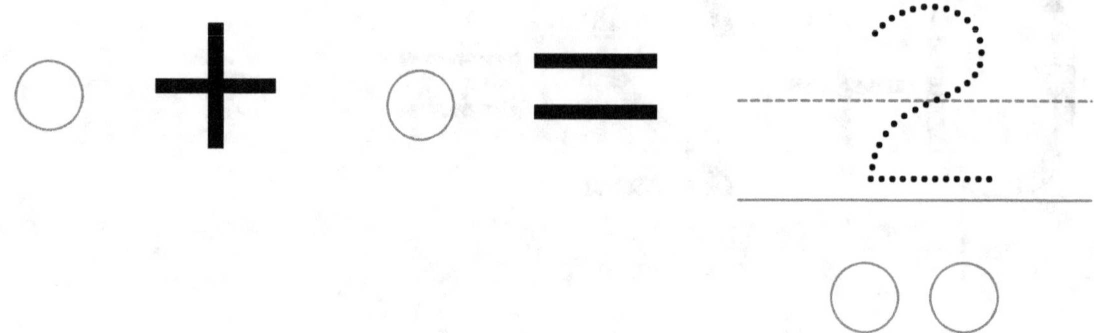

Name

Subtraction: Fill in the blank.

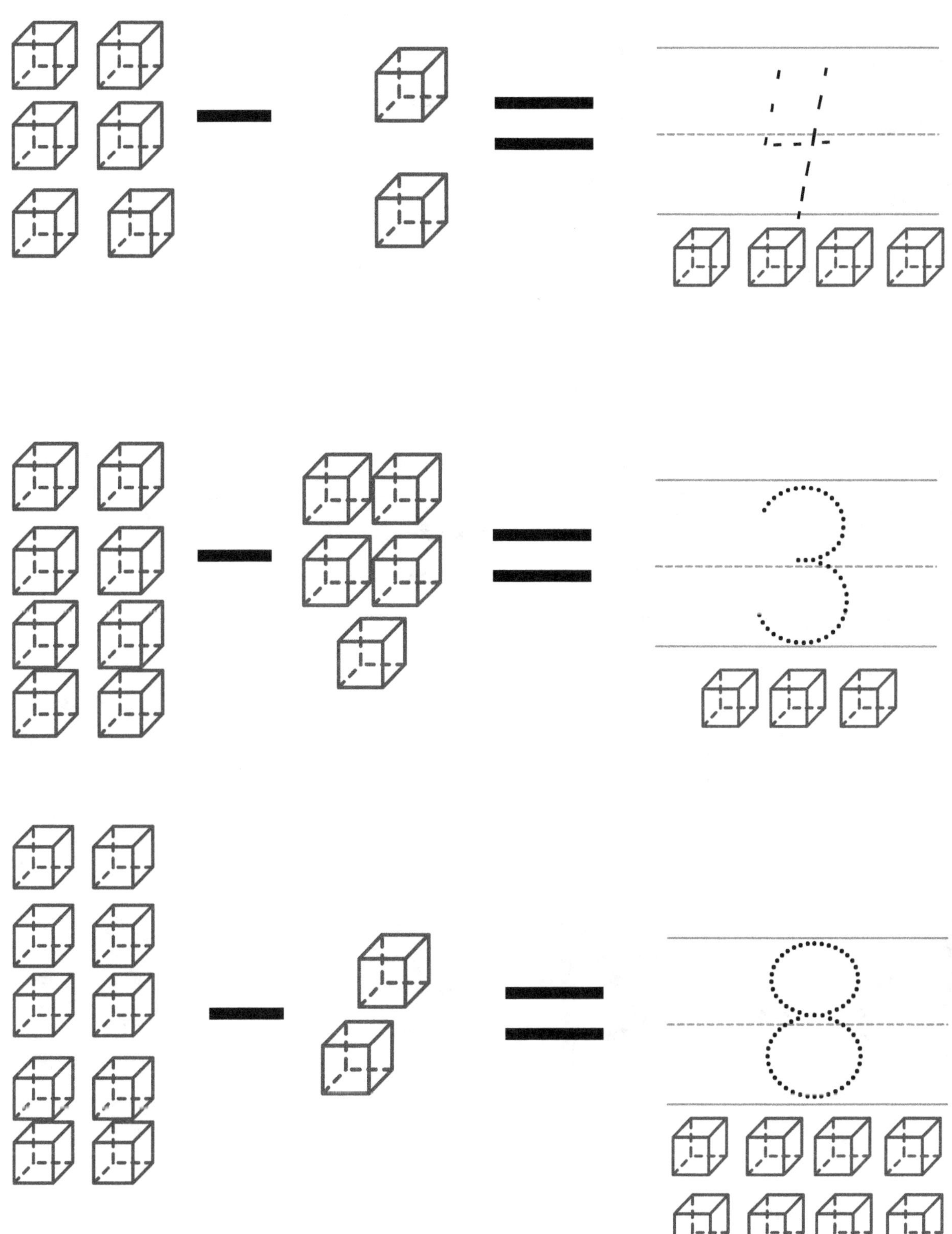

Subtraction: Fill in the blank.

$$3 - 3 = 0$$

$$9 - 2 = 7$$

$$5 - 4 = 1$$

Subtraction: Fill in the blank.

4 - 1 =

2 - 2 =

8 - 4 =

Name

Subtraction: Fill in the blank.

3 - 0 = _______

4 - 3 = _______

6 - 2 = _______

Subtraction: Fill in the blank.

3 - 1 = ______

2 - 1 = ______

7 - 2 = ______

Part 4

Practice, trace, and learn sight words.

Pages 86-97

Name

Trace sight words.

I a is me go

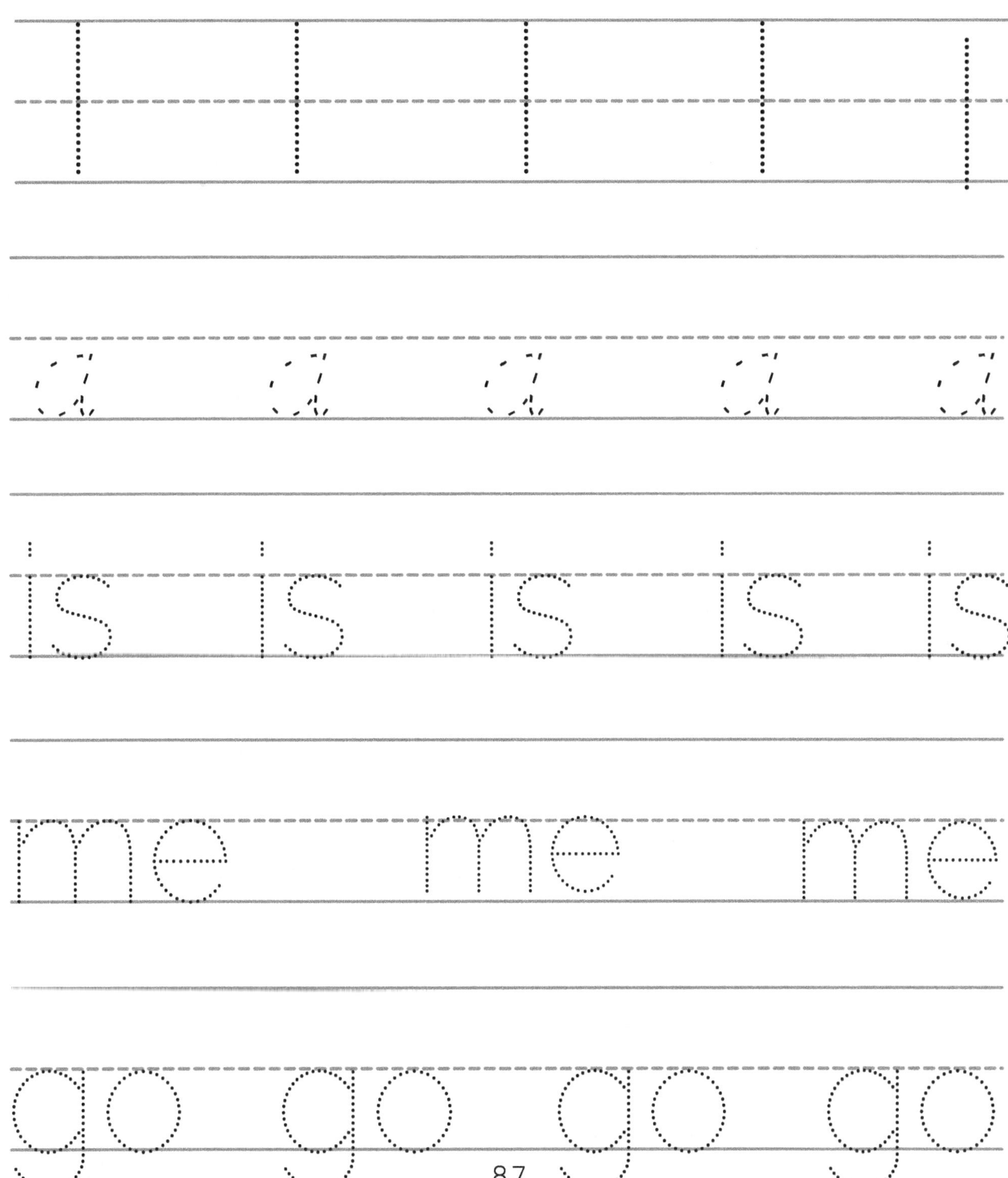

Name

Practice and trace two letter sight words.

we no in do of

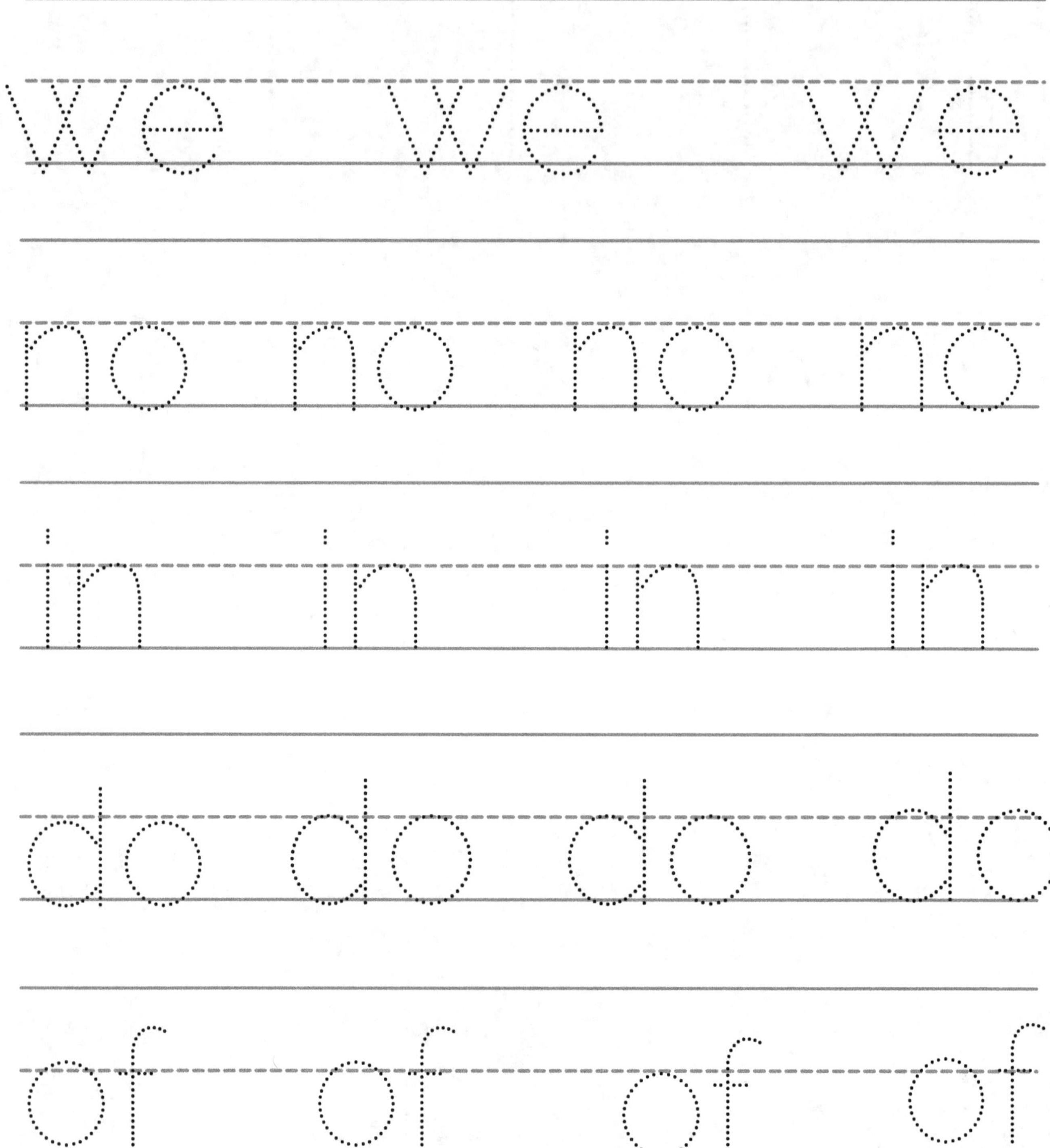

Name

Practice and trace two letter sight words.

it up at my to

it   it   it   it

up   up   up   up

at   at   at   at

my   my   my   my

to   to   to   to

Name

Practice and trace two letter sight words.

be by am so he

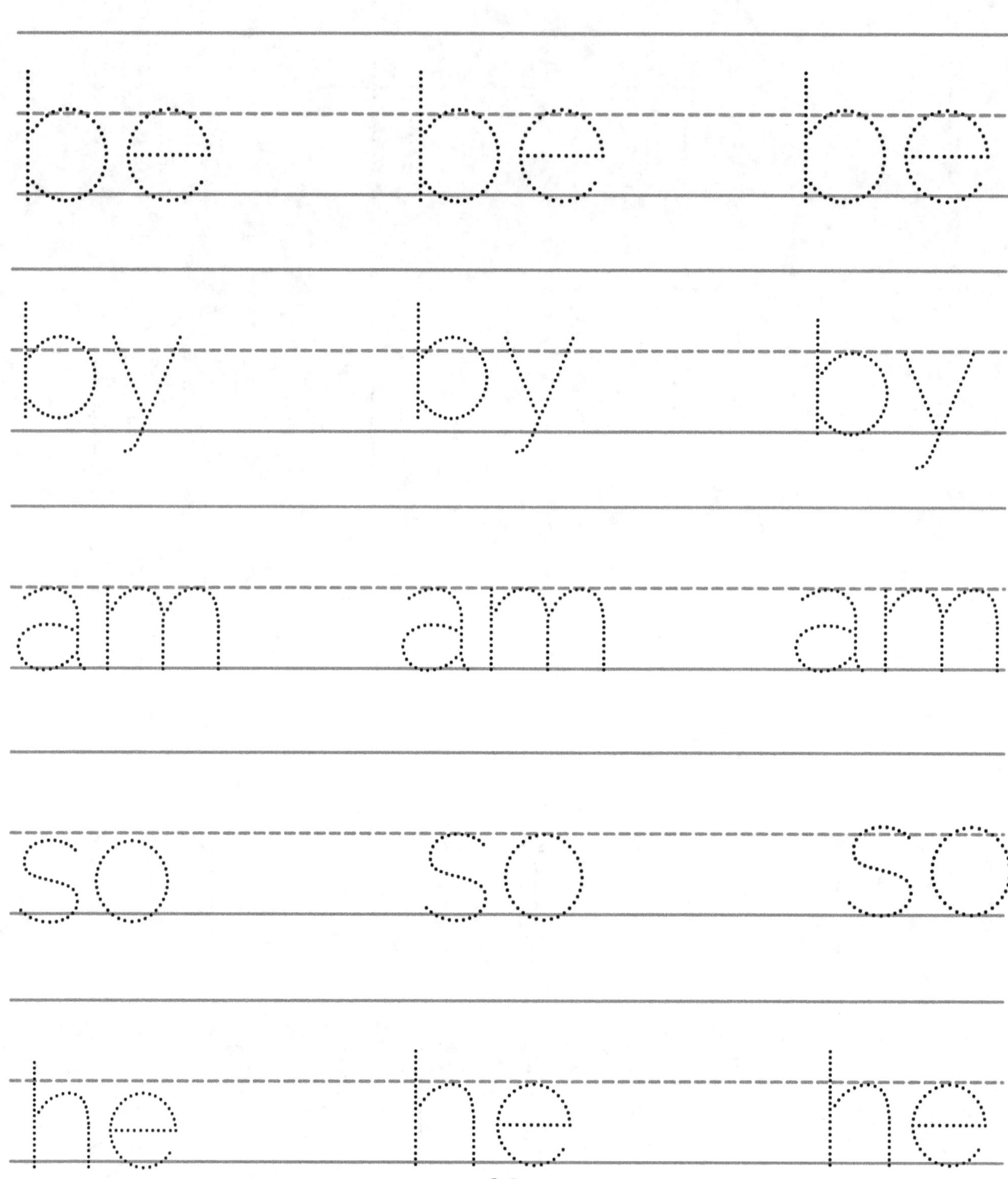

Name

Practice and trace three letter sight words.

big   and   for   the   see

big   big   big

and   and   and

for   for   for

the   the   the

see   see   see

Name _______________

Practice and trace three letter sight words.

run boy cat sun sad

run run run

boy boy boy

cat cat cat

sun sun sun

sad sad sad

Name

Practice and trace three letter sight words.

can   red   dog   one   was

can   can   can

red   red   red

dog   dog   dog

one   one   one

was   was   was

Name _______________

Practice and trace three letter sight words.

old   saw   are   get   sit

old   old   old

saw   saw   saw

are   are   are

get   get   get

sit   sit   sit

Name

Practice and trace three letter sight words.

you   let   eat   who   all

you you you

let   let   let

eat   eat   eat

who   who   who

all   all   all

Name

Practice and trace three letter sight words.

out   not   but   two   six

out   out   out

not   not   not

but   but   but

two   two   two

six   six   six

Name

Practice and trace four letter sight words.

play   blue   down   jump   girl

play play

blue blue

down down

jump jump

girl girl